Awakening the Natural Genius of Black Children

Amos N. Wilson

Awakening the Natural Genius of Black Children

Amos N. Wilson

Afrikan World InfoSystems
New York 1992

First Edition

THIRD PRINTING December 1993

Typesetting and editing by SABABU N. PLATA

Cover design by Joe Gillians

ISBN 1-879164-01-9

AFRIKAN WORLD INFOSYSTEMS
256 East 138 Street,
Bronx, New York 10451

AFRIKAN WORLD INFOSYSTEMS
743 Rogers Avenue, Suite 6
Brooklyn, New York 11226

Printed in the USA

Dedication

In memory of my Parents: Oscar and Lugenia Wilson

To my Sisters: Marjorie, Doris, Teresa and Delores

To my Brothers: Willie C., Albert (late), and Webster

Other Books by Amos N. Wilson

The Developmental Psychology of the Black Child

Black-on-Black Violence: *The Psychodynamics of Black Self-Annihilation in Service of White Domination*

Understanding Black Adolescent Male Violence: *Its Remediation and Prevention*

The Falsification of Afrikan Consciousness: *Eurocentric History, Psychiatry and the Politics of White Supremacy*

About the Author

Professor Amos N. Wilson is a former social case worker, supervising probation officer, psychological counselor, training administrator in the New York City Department of Juvenile Justice, and Assistant Professor of Psychology at the City University of New York. He is currently adjunct Professor of Psychology at The School of New Resources, College of New Rochelle, Co-op City Campus, Bronx, New York.

Contents

Contents

Editor's Note:

The Introductory Lecture, *The Sociopolitical Context Of Education*, was formerly titled Enhancing the Intelligence of the Black Child. It is an excerpt from a lecture delivered under the auspices of the Afrikan Poetry Theater on May 19, 1983, at the Rochdale Community Center, Queens, New York.

Now edited and indexed, we find its contents ever more pertinent in these turbulent times.

In the spirit of Määt we acknowledge the assistance of Nora Ward, Rodney Harris, Charmaine B. Monroe, Carol King and Osei Tutu Rowe, and the inspiratory presence of my daughter Sankofa Ward Plata and my niece Safiya King in the fulfillment of this undertaking.

We anticipate you will find it as edifying as we did.

Sababu N. Plata

THE SOCIOPOLITICAL CONTEXT OF EDUCATION

What is the Purpose of Education?

Too many of us see education as essentially a preparation for jobs, as a preparation for moving up in social status, and as a means of securing a better lifestyle. And certainly, these are some of its major functions. However, I do not see them as the primary functions of education. I think it is vital that we understand that the major function of education is to help secure the survival of a people. When we talk about maximizing the intelligence of Black children we are speaking not just in terms of their ability to go through school and to get better reading and writing averages and go to the right colleges. We are concerned about enhancing their intelligence so that it can serve as a means for maintaining the actual physical survival of Black people. We are now at the crossroads. We are in a pathetic situation as far as the world is concerned. We are in a situation that is exceedingly dangerous, where we are questioning whether Afrikan peoples survive the next century. And consequently, it's going to take a different kind of thinking style, a different system of values, and a different approach to human relations to get us out of this quandary that we are in today; the quandary the European has put us in. And it's going to require a different kind of education than what is available today.

"*You can tell a tree by the fruit it bears.*" Those of us who are familiar with the Bible, of course, are familiar with that

1

verse. We must evaluate education in terms of its fruits. We must evaluate an education that has us at the point today of not knowing when we are going to be blown up; when this world is going to be brought to an end. What kind of civilization is it that as it supposedly becomes more and more civilized becomes more and more deadly?; it becomes less and less able to control itself and it becomes more and more suicidal! It develops weapons and systems that can kill and destroy each man seven hundred times over — if you can die seven hundred times over. Where one nuclear weapon contains the power of all of the bombs dropped in World War II. Just one! And yet we continue to pay taxes to support this system, we continue to admire the people that made this system, continue to want to be "equal" with them, and continue to want to be like them — these people who are threatening to end our lives and our very survival here on earth. They are unworthy of any further leadership on this earth. *They must be replaced for our survival, for the survival of our children, and for the survival of this earth!*

For the Black man to be in the position he is in today, he has to be "out of his mind." We have to be. For a people to vote and pay taxes for weapons that are going to destroy their very lives and the future of their people, they have to be out of their minds. For physicists to build weapons that would end their lives and the lives of their children, they have to be out of their minds. For biologists and for doctors with M.Ds to develop bacteria so that populations can be wiped out by disease, which also means that their own children and their future generations can be wiped out, they must be out of their minds.

For us to sit here and be unaware of what is going on in the world means that we have to be out of touch with reality. And one of the major instruments for putting people out of their minds is education. It is often the very basis for making people ignorant. It is the intellectual and the

Ph.D. that have us in the trouble we're in today. Who do you think builds atomic weapons — the man in the street? No! The physicist who went to school and wanted to be a "Mr. Spock" figure, only concerned with the facts, only concerned with mathematics, only concerned with being objective, only concerned with having an amoral education, only concerned with an education that has no central values, morality, religion.

These scientists are so denuded of morality, love for humanity, and concern for their own children and the generations of their children that they sell their services to the highest bidder and permit themselves to become the tools of politicians.

And this is true for the other professions as well. Isn't it strange that the more social workers and psychologist we produce the crazier we get? The more economists we produce the more our people starve in Afrika? You must recognize that things are backwards. But they must be backwards if a minority of people is to rule over the vast majority. The vast majority must be kept in a state of deception, and they must be even arrogant in their state of ignorance, not open to critical thinking and analysis of their situation.

It has been said that science has done great things for humankind. But when you look at it, it has done great things only for a small percentage of humankind. When you add the population of this country together with the European countries, you've got maybe 20 percent of the earth's population. What's going on with the other 80 percent? The vast majority don't have even indoor plumbing, not even good scientific farming, not any of the conveniences (but maybe a television set so they may be propagandized) that we take for granted.

Do not look at what goes on in the USA and assume that this applies to humankind in general. The greater percentage of the world's wealth is used by a small group of people who have the feeling that they have the right to consume over 60 or 80 percent of the world's energy and resources to maintain their lifestyle.

The Black man must bring into being a new world order. This is the contribution that you can make to America, if you are interested in making a contribution to America. You are not going to make any contribution being a "black-white" man. There are already enough white men for that. The Black man should bring something unique and different to the world. In a sense then, even if we are concerned with the growth and development of America, we should bring something unique and different to it because it is need of something new.

We are faced with *Star Wars*. We are faced with the situation that the Whites are getting ready to leave this planet and no Afrikan nation has yet moved into the position to move our seeds beyond earth. The White man will bomb this planet out of existence but if he can carry one or two of his seeds to the next planet his people will survive. But ours are left here. America has already planted her flag on the moon. Where is the Afrikan flag? Where is the haven for our people when this earth is polluted and destroyed and overrun with radiation? What happens when nuclear warfare, that is sure to come, emits harmful rays and makes mutants of our children?

So when we talk about education we are not just talking about jobs. We are talking about continuing to live and survive in the world of the future. Can we defend ourselves if the weapons of war are going to rain down from thousands of miles out in space? *Can we as an Afrikan people defend your children from re-enslavement any better today than your forefathers defended themselves against enslavement?* Will we see that our strength and our ability to protect ourselves against people who may be our enemy at any point in time is virtually nil? Yet we depend upon the kindness of a people

4

who have mistreated us since the first time we have known them.

We are hanging by a thin thread. The more "integrated" we become, the weaker we become; the more dependent we become. One day when we think we've got it made at the mint, when we are "holding hands with little Black girls and little White girls" — the switch will fall. And then we find out that we are left completely in the open not having prepared at all to deal with the situation. The Jews learned a serious lesson about that: we can be in the universities; we can create an Einstein; we can make great contributions to this society *but that may not keep us from going to the oven.*

The idea that we are going to create children who are going to make great contributions to America is not your salvation. They will have to be in a position to actually defend their lives. Education is a very serious affair for us. It goes beyond the everyday thing of equal opportunity. It is at the very heart of our survival.

We must change the order of things so that while we will not menace the world and will contribute to its peace and security we will not be the clients and the protectorates of others.

Education and the Future of Afrikan Peoples

The world's economic system is moving into a whole new phase and needs this period to restructure the industrial situation, to break the power of unions, to weaken them so that they can replace men and women with robots thus moving in computerized production facilities. More can be produced with fewer people, some industries producing twice as much with much smaller numbers. I remember reading some time ago about a Japanese factory that turned out 1,300 cars a day with a total employment roll of 67 people.

We are facing a future that requires that we get serious about education. Very serious! And not equal education. Brothers and sisters, *the White man's education is not up to par*. If our goal is to have our children read on level with White children, and to attain achievement test scores equal to White children, we are headed for destruction because their best is not good enough.

Read the April 26th, *New York Times* article about, "The Commission on Education." I'm sure some of you are familiar with it. "The tide of mediocrity," they call it, "imperils the U.S. — economically, culturally and spiritually. In an open letter to the American people, the eighteen-member National Education Commission on Excellence in Education, said that "America's economic, cultural and spiritual role in the world is being threatened by lax standards and misguided priorities in the schools." The Commission further intimated that, "The educational foundations of our society are presently being eroded by a rising tide of mediocrity." So you can see why equality should not be your goal. It has got to be superiority. The Black child has got to do better than the White child. Not, as good as. *Better*! Because what they call their best is not good enough. And this is what threatens our very future. You see the article here is talking about what? — *Survival* — not jobs! It is talking about what? — Their very future as a nation and as a people.

The Commission went on to assert, "*If an unfriendly nation had attempted to impose on America the mediocre educational performance that exists today, we might well have viewed it as an act of war.*" Understand what is being said here.

It's hard to make our people understand that we as a people have been in a state of war with Europeans for the last two or three thousand years. We are here as a result of war. We are prisoners of war. Our foreparents were brought here as prisoners of war; and we are still subject to psychological warfare. There is still a major struggle going on between us in this world today. Get what the article says here. "If another country had attempted to impose on America the mediocre educational performance that exists today, we might have viewed it as an act of war." Then what do you think about the mediocre education that is laid upon us? Why is it that I am seen, when I say that we are in a state of war, as being a radical? Education is a form of war. We must understand that every discipline and every institution in this society is a part of its imperialism. Every one! Each is a part of the means by which the European-American intends to maintain dominance over the rest of the world. This includes the churches, the schools, the family, the welfare system, the economic system. You can't name one that isn't. They are all in tandem. Every discipline in our universities is geared towards one end — that of maintaining the dominance of this country. Each is just as much a part of maintaining the dominance of this country, as are its troops and the nuclear weaponry that they have at their hands.

The Board of Education is solely not concerned with education. Education is a *business*. The same thing is true of Corrections. Its principal function seems to be to make criminals out of our imprisoned people. It is an industry. Its millions upon millions of dollars go to the people who sell it the food, to the people that build the prisons, go to the people that sell it electricity, etc. And the raw material of the system are our boys, and our sisters, and our brothers. It [the system] takes the politically weakest groups and processes them so that everyone else gets a piece of them. The cop gets them and he makes his living off of them; then the lawyer gets them, and gets his piece of the action; then the judge gets them; the court officers get them and they hack their piece; they work them right on through the correction system and everybody gets their piece — and the parole officer gets them in the end. By that time they

7

are no good and have got a career going, and they recycle them through it again. It is an industry. It is not about correction. They don't have the philosophy nor the psychology to correct Black people: Nor is it in their interest.

White racists must criminalize and destroy Black men. The Black man must not be permitted to live fully free. Therefore, there are a series of steps that are set up to destroy him along the way. Any system that treats a 13-year-old like any regular adult criminal has admitted that it has failed. And it admits it is going to take your 13-year-old right off the street and put him in prison!

This system depends upon the Black man being down-and-out. Look at the South African situation! It is but an extreme form of what goes on right here. The immigrant South Afrikan man who must live in an all-male compound outside of the city, and who can see his family but once a year; his wife located somewhere living in a shack with their children. That is a system that in order for it to exist must disorganize the Afrikan family. It is the disorganization of the Black family that serves to maintain the South Afrikan system: it is the disorganization of the Black family that serves to maintain this American system.

I was reading a very interesting little book called *Ethnic Enterprises In America*, which compares the economic development of the Chinese, Japanese, and Blacks. And it deals with the issue of — *Why haven't Blacks developed a large or a sizable business class?* Why is it that with over 300 billion dollars in consumer dollars Black people who, if you looked at their income, represent the 9th or 10th richest nation on earth — why is it that they haven't developed a business class? Why is it that they have Asians running their business communities? Why is it that they have other ethnic groups serving their needs? Why is it that they enrich other people and then beg for jobs?" That's an issue we should concern yourselves with. That's an issue at the center of what Black economic education should be

8

about. Not the issue of how do you move up in IBM; a wholly different thing. How do we gain control of those billion of dollars that are available to us and use them for our own interests and for our own advancement?

But, as long as we are in the school trying to learn how to move up in IBM, the Asians are is going to move right in and suck every bit of our nickels and dimes out of our pockets and use them to advance their own interests. At the very point Blacks are getting the most degrees in business we're losing business territory — which tells us that there is something wrong with them. Obviously, these degrees are degrees for servants, which only prepare us to serve the interests of others and not our own. But that is true of any degree. It does not matter what it is. But it must be that way. Do you think the dominant Whites are going to prepare us to fully compete with them?

This is what our education is all about. It's about serious decisions. And this generation of children, must be the one that makes these decisions. Therefore, they must be prepared mentally and their character must be developed so that they can make these major decisions, so that they can lead our people in a way that we can survive in the future. We can seek equal gains and equal jobs and equal opportunity; we can elect all the mayors and governors we want to; and that's good. Go for them. I'm not fighting that. Please do not read this as a discouragement. We should vote every one of them in when we get a chance. But let's not see that as the end-all or the be-all of where we are going, but as a major step to where we are going. Getting in and getting the money that the city represents, getting in and getting the power, getting access to the information and knowledge and transferring that information and knowledge, using it for the advancement of our people so that in the future we'll be in a position to protect our interests throughout the world should be among our ultimate goals.

The Commission on Education went on to say:

Now, the educational foundations of our society are presently being eroded by a rising tide of mediocrity that threatens our very future. What was unimaginable a generation ago has begun to occur. Others are matching and surpassing our educational attainments.

White America is being forced against the wall. We must question every assumption this society puts forward to us. We must not leave any of them unquestioned. We must think the unthinkable and imagine the unimaginable, because those things are going to be the realities of the future.

I mention here a little article just given to me a moment ago. It indicates that a new science city was created to put Japan in the technological lead.

The Japanese have built a high-tech city, the only one of its kind in the world devoted exclusively to advanced-research and development, and designed to propel Japan into prominence in the 21st century.

Here is a country that is essentially nothing but a rock, no resources, just sitting out there and yet it is talking about propelling itself into the 21st century. And it is moving, and it is rich, and yet we look at our Afrikan nations sitting on the wealth of the world and we have to talk about that continent in terms of starvation and poverty. There is something wrong with our economics, psychology and philosophy. Forget Keynes and Adam Smith. Don't be befuddled by names. Look for results! Look at our situation and say, "Our people are starving, our people are poverty-stricken on the wealthiest land in the world. Eurocentric economics and philosophy are not working for us and it is time for us to try new ones. We're not impressed by names." Freud is all right. He's useful, but don't be deceived by him.

Let's look at the psychology of your people. Look at what's going on and evaluate things in terms of the realities of our situation, not in terms of the fame or the prestige of an individual that is putting forth a "great" idea.

Tsukuba Science City has been completed after a dozen years of construction at a cost of four billion dollars spread over seven thousand acres. The man-made metropolis contains two universities, more than fifty government and private research installations populated by 6,500 experts.

This is the use of education. They are not educating their people to work for IBM, or for "equal job opportunities." They are educating their people to have superiority in the world, to deal with the world. And it goes on:

According to far reaching plans in the future, Tsukuba is to be the first of nineteen similar centers to be built throughout the archipelago, each to provide the know-how for various advanced industrial sections. Robots have been developed to take the place of nurses in hospitals. ... and other installations include institutes dealing with research for agriculture, meteorology, geology, textiles, high-energy-disaster prevention. The National Space Development Agency, also located in Tsukuba, has begun to do work on an answer to the United States space-shuttle. Researchers are working with Government subsidies on a program to beat the United States in the development of a 5th generation computer that will operate like a human brain.

This is serious. One of the things I have often said about us is that one of our major problems is that we have no enemies. Japan is not looking for equality; she is looking for superiority. Russia is not looking for equality; she is looking for superiority. Germany is not looking for equality; she is looking for superiority.

The beauty of the White man's system, when viewed in terms of advancing his interests, is not even in education.

It is in the system, the competitive system that he's set up — where they have to compete in order to make it. In the effort of competing they produce for their society. It's the competition that keeps the system going. If we have no one to overcome, then what will motivate us to produce and move forward? Our emphasis has become one of peace — living together, and living on the goodwill of another people hoping somehow we can transform them morally so they won't turn around and do us in — instead of seeing our effort as one of putting ourselves, not on their charity, but of avoiding their charity.

The world is going through cycles. South Korea has grown at a tremendous rate. South Korea is growing faster than Japan. There is Taiwan, Hong Kong and other areas. This raises a major question as to whether (when this cycle peaks) we are going to be subjected to two or three thousand years of Asian domination! When European civilization declines, who is coming up next? The Asians and Arabs? Or, when this cycle ends, *does this mean that it will be time for the Afrikan nations to rise, for Afrikan people to rise and be in control of their own destiny?* Or, are we going to be tailing again another group of people for how many more hundreds or maybe thousands of years, as we have now permitted ourselves to be the tail on the European dog? That's an issue that our children have got to face and deal with. And the Asians are not going to be anymore sympathetic to us than are the Europeans, as I am sure many of us are already beginning to learn.

The education of our children is too serious for us to leave it in the hands of other people. We can't just turn our children over at will and give them away. We can't unwittingly take other people's advice about how to rear and deal with our children. They are always going to set things up in ways that work to their advantage, even when they have good intentions.

The Developmental Potential of the Black Child

The Black child is born with great, great potential. We have indicated in the book, *The Developmental Psychology of the Black Child*, that *"the Black child is not a white child 'painted' black."* In the Black child *Afrikan heritage* means something. The Black man being the first man to walk this earth, to establish civilizations, to build institutions, governments and so forth, I think is still genetically represented in the Black child.

We now quote the following from *The Developmental Psychology of the Black Child*:

Comparison of African and European Psychomotor Development

1. Nine (9) hours old being drawn up in a sitting position, able to prevent its head from falling backward; it takes the European child (six) 6 weeks.
2. Two (2) days old, with head held firmly, looking in the face of the examiner; the European child eight (8) weeks.
3. Seven (7) weeks old, supporting herself in a sitting position and watching her reflection in the mirror; the European child twenty (20) weeks.
4. Five (5) months old, holding herself upright; the European child nine (9) months.
5. Five (5) months old, taking the round block out of its hole in the form board; the European child takes eleven (11) months. Five (5) months old, standing against the mirror; it takes the European child nine (9) months.
6. Seven (7) months old, walking to the Gesell Box to look inside; it takes the European child fifteen (15) months.
7. Eleven (11) months old, climbing the steps alone; the European child takes fifteen (15) months.[1]

---

[1] Wilson, Amos N. *The Developmental Psychology of the Black Child.* New York: Africana Research Publications, 1978. pp. 46

13

The differences in Afrikan and European heritages are responsible for these developmental differences. This is why we have to look at Afrika as the source of understanding the development of our children — not Europe.

It is the use of Europeans as our standard of measure that has turned Black psychology into a psychology of deviancy, which makes us talk about our children in terms of deviances, deficiencies, as slow learners, and in other kinds of negative ways. We are using the wrong standard of measurement.

One of the major things necessary for enhancing the intelligence of our children is to have knowledge of their development. It has been shown clearly that it is not so much the income, but a knowledge of how our children develop that is very important to their intellectual development. Our lack of knowledge about the development of our children helps to retard the intellectual potential that our children so abundantly possess. If we use European developmental scales we may be waiting too late since their children develop later than our own. We must gear the education of our children to their developmental rates. Because our children are growing at different rates and in different ways compared to whites they must have different standards for meeting their nutritional needs. All of these things point to the need for us to have a sound knowledge of the Afrikan child.

It is not what we've got, it is not the status of the parents that is important, but it's what we parents do that is most important for enhancing the intelligence of our children. Much of what we need does not require money. Interest, motivation, dedication is what we need. We can make various toys out of empty boxes. We can give a child pots and pans to play with, anything to develop its discrimination and to develop its coordination, to develop the feel for objects. To develop many of its abilities we can go to the park and classify flowers, we can pick up rocks and teach categorization. We can hunt butterflies, or bees, or anything: all of which can become a basis for scientific thought development. We can look in store windows and talk about colors. We can use things all around us.

Infant Stimulation The nature of the home environment at six months can give us some indication of how the infant's mind is going to be at three and four years old. The emotional nature of the home, the emotional responses of the mother, the parental involvement of the mother with the child, the provision of appropriate play materials, are very important to the child's development. Play things are very important. Give them something to see, touch, draw, manipulate, hit, to rattle. All those things are important for growth and development.

The Japanese are surpassing the Europeans and their IQ is growing. *Discover* magazine, September 1982, asked the following question — *"IQ Are The Japanese Really Smarter?"* White Americans are asking themselves this question. That sounds like our question, doesn't it? It is amazing to see them in this predicament. Because they told us that IQ is innate. When they tested the Japanese back in the 1940s the average scores were basically the same. But what shocks them is that in 1983, the Japanese average score is 15 points above that of the average White American. Japanese IQ has grown, and they are wondering if it is going to keep growing. When they [Whites] told us [Blacks] that their average score was 15 points above ours they swore that intelligence is inborn and natural! What are they going to say now? That the Japanese are naturally, innately smarter? No! They are not admitting that now. When you read this article you read them saying, "Let's look at the schools, let's see how they are being educated." They present all the comparisons of how much time White children stay in class as compared to the Japanese. In fact, a part of this educational report suggests that Americans must get our

15

children to stay in school longer because the Japanese stay in school longer. So we see all those environmental arguments that we had put forward in the defense of our intelligence, that they so valiantly resisted, they themselves are using now that they are in the very same position. "We must restructure the schools; we must restructure the family; we must restructure the value system"; because all of a sudden they find all these things are important to the intellectual growth and advancement of their children.

Language Development Black children are psychomotorically ahead of White children until they get to about age three. The major reason why they start falling behind at age three, and particularly five, is because their way of dealing with the world shifts. Up to about age two or three, the major way of dealing with the world is to deal with it concretely, i.e., through the ability to handle objects, to coordinate the body and psychophysical systems. But at around the age of three, the way of dealing with the world is increasingly by the word, and it is at that point that our children begin to slip because they do not use words and language as proficiently as they should. We may brag about how we are able to dance and throw basketballs, but in the end it is not the throwing of the basketballs that determines power in the world. It is the ability to use words and symbols. One of the other reasons why our children remain stuck intellectually is that we were brought to this world, the "New World" — and the function of the Afrikans the world-over is — to be servants to Europeans. Therefore we tend to think like servants. Our ability to think abstractly is detrimental to European interests. If we want to know the characteristics that White racism wishes to impose on the Black child (and on Black people in general) there is one major question we may ask yourselves. What is it that we must not be able to do or have in our character if the White man is to stay dominant? And we will see those

16

characteristics missing or impaired in many of us and our children. For Afrikan people must not think abstractly because we may see through his [the White oppressor's] game. We must not think logically and relationally; everything must be immediate and concrete or we may see the games that he is running on us. If the Europeans are to continue to dominate us, certain intellectual, social, emotional-behavioral and organizational abilities must be repressed in Afrikan children; the ability to read and understand language profoundly must be reduced. The White man is so arrogant that he puts his knowledge right in front of our face most often in written form. He doesn't keep us from going to libraries, he doesn't keep us from reading, he doesn't keep us from buying books. But he has so manipulated our interest and motivation, has put us in such a state that he can place written and other forms of information right before our eyes and we will not look at and understand them. And every means by which the White man rules us is written in books — every one of them. But we are not going to see them. *We read about the rat in the Skinner box and don't know we are the rat in the box. We read about Pavlov's dog and we don't know that we are the dog!* We read how he (the White man) controls consciousness: he has whole chapters on consciousness, how people are put under hypnosis, how to propagandize people. All of these methods are in books. The White imperialist does not hide them from us at all. Because he knows that our mentality is twisted in such a way he has little need to do so. Because he has reduced early in our lives the ability to read between the lines. He has reduced our ability to go beyond what we see. He has reduced early in our lives our intense desire to pursue *sequential-thinking* and *implications*; to read something and to ask what does it mean for the future? Or he reduces early in our lives our ability or desire to look in the past, connect it with the present, and project it into the future. We live for the moment.

17

But we must connect the past and the present, we must be able to look at what's going on in the present and project probabilities as to what is going to happen in the future. Our ability to project into the future permits us to act on the present so as to influence the future; to say, 'Well, looking at the way things are going, the way the current interactions are taking place, I see a future that I don't want. And since I see a future that I don't want, let me change the nature of this interaction so that it can bring about a world that I do want.'

One of the most important ways of breaking the reins of concrete thinking is through the expanded use of language. With expanded language we can mentally travel the world. With language we go into the fourth dimension. With language we can fly in space, we go anywhere we want to go. With symbols we create anything that we want to create. Let's turn our children on to symbols. See that they learn word-meanings. See that they know how to ask questions and deal with questions. Give them aspirations and expectations. One of the reasons our children do not grow as much as they can is because we do not expect them to grow to their fullest extent. Our children are born with the best brains in the world and they can deal with any kind of problem that we put to them. Any kind of problem that we must solve, whether it is science, technology, mathematics or whatever — they can solve! We did it in Egypt! We don't need any proof of our capability of doing it! Our people were among the first to invent mathematics, so when we practice it we are practicing our heritage. But if we believe Black people are not good in math, then, of course, we are going to produce exactly what we believe. If we expect and can believe then we can produce whatever we will — but we must believe.

18

Bibliography

Furth, Hans G. and Wachs, Harry. *Thinking Goes To School: Piaget's Theory In Practice*. New York: Oxford University Press, 1975.

Koch, Jaroslav. *Total Baby Development*. New York: Pocket Books, 1976.

Light, Ivan H. *Ethnic Enterprises In America: Business and Welfare Among Chinese, Japanese, and Blacks*. Los Angeles: University of California Press, 1973.

Verny, Thomas and Kelly, John. *The Secret Life of The Unborn Child*. New York: Summit Books, 1981.

White, Burton L. *The First Three Years of Life: A guide to the physical, emotional, and intellectual growth of your baby*. New York: Avon Books, 1975.

Wilson, Amos N. *The Developmental Psychology of the Black Child*. New York: Africana Research Publications, 1978.

Awakening the Natural Genius of Black Children

Introduction

This volume is about the relationship between intelligence and experience, how the latter helps to shape and direct the former. The very essence of intelligence involves the use of pre-existing abilities and capabilities, past experience, contemporary circumstances and anticipated events in order to achieve intended goals or to resolve a problem. Intelligence is grounded in experience. Experiences, past, present and anticipatory, are the precursory materials out of which intelligence is dynamically constructed and which intelligence interrelatedly processes in order to accomplish certain adaptive goals. Therefore, the quantity and quality of experience, both as precursor and as contemporary "raw material," markedly influences the development, character and manifest expression of what we refer to as intelligence or intelligent behavior.

The quality and variety of learning experiences which occur during infancy and early childhood are the most important factors which determine the character and power of later intelligence.

The most important sources of the kinds of experience which form the infrastructure of intelligence are those which are the product of the social/educational interactions the child has with its caregivers and its psychosocial and physical environments. Environmental interaction is the engine which drives human development on all levels, including the development of human intelligence. J. McVicker Hunt, author of *Intelligence and Experience*, corroborates this assertion when he concludes that "development doesn't come just from exposure to the environment. It comes from the child's attempt to cope with his environment — from his *experiences* in acting on the things and people around him and getting a response from them."[1]

Hunt, (1979) the foremost scholar on intelligence and its relationship to experience, intimates that on the average, people's intelligence can be raised "by about 30 to 35 points of the IQ." He contends furthermore that:

> ...the range is actually much greater than that [the 30 to 35 points of IQ just mentioned]. Intelligence drops by about 50 points for children who are reared from birth in extremely monotonous and unresponsive conditions, as in some orphanages, and it can go up by 25 to 30 points — even for children of mentally retarded mothers — when children are reared in a high-powered educational day-care center from a few months after birth. That would give you a 75-point range of reaction. We could probably go up another 10 to 15 points if we had a better understanding of the kinds of experience that are most important at every stage.

In referring to his research with "five successive waves of infants [who were residents in orphanages in Iran] offering each group a different set of experiences," Hunt notes that each set of experiences brought about a corresponding set of completely different and surprisingly specific results. After devising several different approaches for stimulating each group of babies, Hunt describes some results he obtained from the final group for which he designed a specific program.

> Then we devised a new program to foster language development, as well as other kinds of learning, for our final wave of 11 infants. This is when we got really unexpected, serendipitous results... .
>
> A tremendous change in behavior, in initiative. They looked so different from all the others. They had a verve! Always gesturing or doing something... .
>
> The last wave of infants we worked with ... scored higher than many middle-class kids in our tests, however. At 18 months

of age, they all spoke more than 50 words, and by 22 months, were spontaneously naming objects. Furthermore, they reached the top steps on five of our seven scales of psychological development at a somewhat earlier age than did home-reared infants from largely professional families in Worcester, Mass.

The program Hunt describes was apparently "wholistic" in its effect in that its results seem to have positively pervaded the whole personalities of the children, not just their intellectual character. He notes that while he expected that the program would produce improvements...

I did not expect the change in the children's facial expression, initiative, and sense of trust. They had become extremely attractive children.

They expected people to help them get what they wanted; they acted as if they felt in control of their lives, and this seems to have come from the caretakers' responsiveness during the vocal games. At the same time, these babies had formed the early learning set that "things have names." As a result, they took charge of building their vocabularies, became highly attentive to language, and also very verbal.

We have quoted Hunt at length here because his research so dramatically illustrates the remarkably subtle but powerful influence interactive experience has on the growth and development of intelligence and on the personality in general. His, and the research of many other developmental psychologists, illustrate furthermore that newborns and infants are remarkably responsive to their environments and are extremely capable processors of information, learners and talented actors. At birth children bring with them marvelous intellectual potential and learning instruments. However, that potential and those instruments must be stimulated, exercised and challenged if they are to be maximally developed and utilized. This can best be accomplished when we recognize the intelligence that the newborn and infant possesses and match its capabilities and needs with appropriate psychosocial and material stimuli.

A cursory review of developmental psychological research during the past 25 years is most impressive in what it reveals about the learning and problem solving capacities of newborns and infants. We think the brief review outlined below clearly shows why the nature of the child's social and material environment is so influential, for better or worse, on its later personality and intellectual character.

- Infants are capable of associative learning from the early days of their lives. For example, only after one-half hour of training, infants as young as 2 to 4 days old have been taught to discriminate between two different stimuli, e.g., two different sounds, in order to obtain a desirable reward such as a taste of sugar water.
- Six-week-old infants can demonstrate remarkably good memories. Two weeks after a six-week-old infant had learned to move a mobile with its arm or leg it remembered which limb to move even though the limb was not attached to the mobile as it was at the beginning.
- There is evidence that babies may be born with or acquire in the first days of their lives the ability to imitate the facial gestures of adults. One researcher reports that forty infants younger than 3 days old and one as young as 42 minutes old clearly imitated the gestures of their adult caretakers.
- It has been demonstrated that some infants as young as 1 year can imitate up to three different actions they had seen the day before, implying that deferred imitation (and relatively long-term memory) may occur much earlier than previously thought. Deferred imitation indicates that the infant can recognize objects and actions related to them and after a delay can imitate

those actions (within limits) based on stored memories and active recall.

- By 1½ years old, many infants are capable of reflecting upon themselves and their actions and demonstrate an emerging notion of themselves or an emerging self-concept.

- Infants as young as 9 months old or younger are very sensitive to their mother's mood. It has been shown that the mother's moods can actually influence the infant's behavior as well as its emotional expressions (which may reflect those of the mother's).

- New evidence suggests that the infant's senses are to some practical degree interrelated at birth or that the infant learns to integrate their activities rather soon thereafter.

- Infants turn their head to look at the source of a sound from birth. By 4 months they can match a sound to the most appropriate of two simultaneous visual displays. One-month-old infants have demonstrated that they can visually recognize objects they previously had only felt in their mouths.

- Some researchers have presented evidence which suggests that infants as young as 6 months can perceive casual relations among moving objects in ways qualitatively similar to or the same as adults.

- Infants as young as 6 to 7 months whose parents use sign language have been observed to begin to use conventional signs around that time. Deaf babies of deaf parents have been observed to "babble" with their hands in a rhythmic, repetitive fashion similar to the vocal babbling of hearing infants.

- There is experimental evidence that infants between 3 and 5 months begin to think about or to "contemplate" objects. At 6 months, if not earlier, they have been observed to intensely examine objects.

- Infants at 4 months seem to meaningfully compare and contrast one object with another. At 8 months as if engaged in a comparison process they may visually switch back and forth between two objects many times.
- As early as 3 months infants may differentiate biological (live creatures) from non-biological (mechanical) motion.
- The infant's auditory system is functioning in the womb. Soon after birth the infant is able to process and make sense of sounds as demonstrated by research which indicates that newborns, within the first few hours after birth can tell certain sounds apart.
- Recent research has demonstrated that babies are systematic listeners. One-month-old infants have been observed to discriminate between two sounds as close together as "bah" and "pah."
- Through "discriminative sucking" 3-day-old infants have demonstrated that they could tell their mother's voice from that of other women.
- In homes where parents talked to their children frequently, almost from birth (i.e., where they shared excitement over some event or discovery) the children tend to develop impressive linguistic abilities.
- Since children demonstrate a capacity to understand simple words and instructions usually between 6 and 8 months old we also may infer that they must have established some kind of conceptual system that time.
- The general consensus in developmental psychology is that the greatest difference in the intellectual, psychological and social prospects of young children can be made during the first 3 years of their lives, the time during which the foundation upon which later development is constructed.[2]

The relationship between the sensory/conceptual information processing capacities of newborns and infants and their later intellectual development is substantiated by developmental studies demonstrating that infants' performance on tests of visual memory at ages 4 and 6 months correlate significantly with their IQ at 4 and 6 years of age. Visual memory tests are based on *habituation*, an early form of learning which seems to indicate that newborns have a mind quite capable of performing rather sophisticated mental operations. Habituation, which is frequently used to gauge the functioning of infants' brains and nervous systems and as a measure of the infant's maturity and well-being, becomes increasingly operational over the first 2½ months of life. The basic learning and memory processes it indicates in newborns and infants are based on the finding that babies tend to look longer at new objects or listen longer to a new sound than at or to ones they have seen or heard several times in a row before or are already familiar with. Habituation thus implies that infants remember having seen or heard the object or sound before and can discriminate between those familiar stimuli and new ones. Thus, the capacity of the infant to perform discriminately, to store and recall information, to focus its attention on new and exciting stimuli and encode some form of useful information in regard to them seems to be operationally present at, if not before, birth. More importantly, the perceptual and related information processing capacities of infants are no doubt stimulated by and responsive to various types of environmental stimuli. And interactions with various stimuli are encoded, recorded, retrieved, and to some primitive degree, conceptually utilized by infants in ways which help them to intelligently adapt to and operate on their world. With appropriate experience, appropriate transitional and novel changes in the levels of complexity of stimulation, the adaptational and operational intelligence of the child exhibits commensurate growth and power. Within carefully defined limits, the maximization of one stimulates the maximization of the other.

The Afrikan child is in no way psychologically, physically, or mentally less prepared by nature to undertake the tasks of intellectual development than are children who are members of any other ethnic group. Afrikan children's intellectual potential is second to none. In fact, neonatal and early childhood research not only definitely indicate that the Afrikan child's intellectual and behavioral capacities are the equal of the child from any other ethnic group but they may be significantly more advanced. That is, Black children seem to have been given a "natural head start" in intellectual and behavioral abilities. Preliminarily, a few comments regarding the intellectual and behavioral development of Afrikan children compared to that of European children offered by Chilton Pearce (speaking of research performed by Geber) may be enlightening at this juncture:

I have mentioned that Marcelle Geber spent one year doing long-term studies of 300...home-delivered infants in Uganda. She used the famous Gesell tests for early intelligence, developed at Yale University's child development center. The pictures of the forty-eight-hour-old child — supported only by the forearms, bolt upright, perfect head balance and eye focus, and a marvelous intelligence shining in the face — are no more astonishing than those of the six-week-old child. At six or seven weeks, all 300 of these children crawled skillfully, could sit up by themselves, and would sit spellbound before a mirror looking at their own images for long periods. This particular ability was not to expected in the American-European child before twenty-four weeks (six *months*) according to the Gesell tests. Between six and seven months, the Ugandan children performed the toy-box retrieval test. Geber showed the infant a toy, walked across the room, put the toy in a tall toy box; the child leaped up, ran across the room, and retrieved the toy. Besides the sensorimotor skills of walking and retrieval, the test shows that object constancy has taken place, the great shift of logical processing in the brain, at which point an object out of sight is no longer out of mind... This test, successfully completed by the Ugandan children between six and seven months of age, was not to be expected until somewhere between the fifteenth and sixteenth months in the American and European child.[3]

The developmental differences to which Pearce refers are apparently generally true of children of Afrikan descent across all important developmental areas. Thus, the Afrikan child enters the world well equipped to intelligently interact with the world and to mature intellectually, socially and spiritually as a result thereof. However, the unparalleled inherent or natural readiness of Afrikan children must be matched with a sufficiently stimulating socially and materially interactive environment if their enormous intellectual and human potentials are to be realized. Positive attitudes towards them and their future, high expectations regarding their ability to achieve whatever goals they set for themselves, knowledge of their unique developmental psychology, the freedom and ability to provide them with the necessary social, cultural, material and spiritual resources; an Afrikan-centered consciousness and identity and high personal/cultural/moral aspirations, are the ingredients which when proportionately combined, can maximize all their positive abilities.

It is our hope that this volume will serve as a useful guide to fully enhancing the rich intellectual and human potential of Afrikan children for Afrikan American parents, care-givers, and all other professionals and paraprofessionals who may be concerned with the development and education of Afrikan American children. Of course, a book of this size can only be suggestive. However, we believe that the guidelines and references it provides can be utilized by the reader to develop fairly detailed and practical approaches to maximizing the intelligence of Afrikan children.

The concerns and recommendations of this book which began with an edited speech by the author followed by reviews of child rearing, parent-training, and early childhood educational approaches which have been experimentally demonstrated to significantly maintain and boost the intellectual performance of Afrikan American children, covers the years from birth to approximately six years old — the preschool years. We recommend that the reader follow this book up by reading the companion books by the author, *The Developmental Psychology of the Black Child* and the soon-to-be-published *Educating The Afrikan Child for the 21st Century: A Rationale for an Afrikan-centered Curriculum* (working title). The latter book will critically examine the nature of the contemporary miseducation of Afrikan children and people and review methods used and make recommendations for improving their academic achievement from preschool to pre-college. We think these three volumes may provide the interested reader with a sound intellectual and practical framework and set of reference points for actualizing the enormous intellectual potential of our children.

Notes

1. Pines, M. 1979. "A Head Start in the Nursery." *Psychology Today*, Sept. pp. 56-68.

2. Articles which cite the research studies which are the bases for the above developmental milestones include:—
    Trotter, R. 1987. "You've Come A Long Way, Baby." *Psychology Today,* May 21, No 5, pp. 34-44.
    Mandler, J. 1990. "A New Perspective on Cognitive Development in Infancy." *American Scientist, 78*, No. 3, May-June, pp. 236-243.

3. Pearce, J. 1980. *Magical Child*, New York: Bantam, Books, pp. 68-69.

Chapter 1

The Psychomotor Potential of the Black Child

The Sensorimotor Foundation of IQ

It is a truism, as intimated by Pearce (1980) that: "the growth of intelligence, rests on a sensorimotor process, a coordination of the child's muscular system with his sensory system and general brain processes." Both physical and mental development are founded on the child's body movements, related sensory contacts and interactions with a world of objects, relations, and processes. Pearce further insinuates that:

> The early child thinks in action and acts his thinking. Intellectual growth is a biological process, taking place below awareness as nonconsciously as the growth of hair or teeth. Our conscious awareness is the end product of biological functions. The infant-child learns from every interaction, and all future learning is based on the character of these early, automatic body-brain patterns. This primary sensory organization and response takes precedence over all future learning, even though it never becomes conscious in any ordinary sense. Rather, this base structure furnishes consciousness as well as the possibilities for further learning.[1]

The child's physical and attentional contacts with the world are the sources of a corresponding patterning, dynamic structuring, or learning in his very impressionable brain. Sensory feedback from these contacts and the

31

intentional reactions actions (feed forward) they provoke and the dynamic brain patterns which reflect them, help to establish the child's structure of knowledge, his cognitive-behavioral orientation and world view. To quote Pearce (1980) again in this regard:

> The story of development for the first four or five years is the structuring of these brain patterns from sensory experience and the resulting feedback and synthesis that take place within the brain.
>
> * * *
>
> All thinking arises out of concreteness, which means out of the brain patterns resulting from actual body movements of interacting with actual things. But thinking then moves toward autonomy, that is, moves toward independence of those concrete patterns or physical principles. This progression toward pure thought is itself genetically programmed and unfolds in neat sequential stages.

The sensorimotor basis of intelligence is substantially demonstrated by the empirical relationship between infants' habituation behavior and response to novelty or novelty preference and intelligence as measured by the IQ score. Habituation refers to the tendency of infants (and adults) to pay visual and other sensory-based attention to a repeatedly presented stimulus for progressively shorter time periods and then to, pay visual and sensory-based attention to a new or novel stimulus for a substantially longer time period. Habituation is the process of "getting used to" certain stimuli (Papalia and Olds, 1985). Rapid habituation behavior among new born infants has been found to substantially correlate with a higher verbal IQ, greater persistence and higher Stanford-Binet test scores at age five compared to infants who evidence rather slower habituation behavior (Sigman, M., Cohen, S. Beckwith, B. and Topinka, (1986).[2] Novelty preference appears to be substantially correlated to verbal as well as overall IQ. As stated by Storfer (1990) response to novelty samples a different aspect of cognitive functioning than that measured by habituation-behavior. He indicates that:

> Novelty response requires successful visual or auditory retention and recognition (re-identification, based on effective discrimination at "encoding"), as well as a motivational interest in attending closely when a novel object or sound is presented.

The typical habituation-novelty preference experiment proceeds as follows:

> One test involves showing infants photographs or pictures and measuring how long they look at them. In theory, babies will look at a new stimulus for a longer time than one they remember having seen before. Babies that are likely to be below average in intelligence will remember fewer of the stimuli they have never seen before.[3]

Utilizing this and similar experimental procedures for testing the relationships between visual, auditory and tactile responsiveness and intelligence as measured by IQ tests, Fagan and associates (1981, 1983) and other researchers have shown that the habituation and novelty responses (particularly visual responses) of infants as young as four to six months of age correlate substantially with their scores on IQ tests four to six years later. Those correlations while by no means absolute, indicate that visual memory is already linked to IQ during infancy and is related in some fundamental way to the nature of intelligence (Rose, Feldman, and Wallace, 1988).[4] While the relationship between habituation and novelty preference and IQ may be genetically structured there is evidence that these behaviors are subject to environmental influence, implying that they can be taught in infancy (and later) and enhanced in such ways as to become a permanent part of an individual's intellectual infrastructure (Bornstein, (1985).[5] Ruddy and Bornstein (1982)[6] and Bornstein (1985) found a strong association between maternal encouragement of attention at four and thirteen months and intellectual performance at four years of age. Thus, it appears that sensorimotor efficiency and competence in interaction with the environment (including social mediation by caregivers and significant others) contribute very significantly to the development of intellectual-behavioral character and power.

The Black Child, Sensorimotor and Brain Power

If the growth of intelligence is rooted in the sensorimotor process then the Afrikan-Afrikan American child enters the world very well-equipped to develop an intelligence that is of the highest quality and power. In terms of *psycho*motor abilities and development, the Afrikan child begins its life with a natural and definite head start. Numerous studies have found that children of Afrikan descent achieve sensory, motor, and intellectual milestones well in advance of their White counterparts. Pearce (1980) testifies this advancement in his review of the work of Marcelle Geber in Kenya and Uganda:

[In] 1956, Marcelle Geber, under a research grant from the United Nations Children's Fund, traveled to Africa to study the effects of malnutrition on infant and child intelligence ... and made a momentous discovery. She found the most precocious, brilliant, and advanced infants and children ever observed anywhere. These infants had smiled, continuously and rapturously, from, at the latest, their fourth day of life. Blood analyses showed that all the adrenal steroids connected with birth stress were totally absent by the fourth day after birth. *Sensorimotor learning and development were phenomenal, indeed miraculous. A superior intellectual development held for the first four years of life.*

... These infants were awake a surprising amount of time — alert, watchful, happy, calm. They virtually never cried. The mother responded to the infant's every gesture and assisted the child in any and every move that was undertaken, so that every move initiated by the child ended in immediate success. *At two days of age (forty-eight hours) these infants sat bold upright, held only by the forearms, with a beautifully straight back and perfect head balance, their finely focused eyes staring intently, intelligently at their mothers.* And they smiled and smiled.[7] (Emphasis mine).

These Afrikan infants exhibited the very traits, e.g., alertness, attentiveness, social "interactiveness", curiosity, upright body position, etc., which are the bases for accelerated and enhanced intellectual development (Storfer, 1990; Ludington-Hoe, 1987). Intellectual growth in infancy results from the increased ability of the infant to interact with his world and internalize experience through the smoothly coordinated interaction of mind, brain and body. That this interaction of brain and body is well within the purview of Afrikan children is again corroborated by Pearce's (1980) description of Geber's (1958) work with Afrikan children:

She [Marcelle Geber] used the famous Gesell tests for early intelligence, developed at Yale University's child development center. The pictures of the forty-eight-hour-old child—supported only by the forearms, bolt upright, perfect head balance and eye focus, and a marvelous intelligence shining in the face—are no more astonishing than those of the six-week-old child. *At six or seven weeks...*these children crawled skillfully, could sit up by themselves, and would sit spellbound before a mirror looking at their own images for long periods. *This particular ability was not to be expected in the American-European child before twenty-four weeks (six months)* according to the Gesell tests. Between six and seven months, the Uganda children performed the toy-box retrieval test. Geber showed the infant a toy, walked across the room, put the toy in a tall toy box; the child leaped up, ran across the room, and retrieved the toy. Besides the sensorimotor skills of walking and retrieval, the test shows that object constancy has taken place, the first great shift of logical processing in the brain, at which point an object out of sight is no longer out of mind (the characteristic of infancy and early childhood). *This test, successfully completed by the Ugandan children between six and seven months of age, was not to be expected until somewhere between the fifteenth and eighteenth months in the American and European child.*[8] (Emphasis added)

Studies of Kikuyu infants performed by Leiderman and associates (1973)[9] corroborate these findings by Geber. These children of the Kikuyu people, who live some 25 miles from Nairobi, Kenya were tested and examined in accordance with the Bayley scales of infant development. These scales which have been thoroughly standardized with large populations of infants in the U.S. and used extensively in Europe and other countries, consist of two parts: a physical scale which assesses physical maturation; and a mental scale, which assesses perceptual and sensory functions. Jackson and Jackson (1978) describe the Kikuyu infants thusly:

On both the mental and motor tests, the Kikuyu infants were precocious, scoring significantly higher than would be expected for American infants of the same ages. As compared with the standard score of 100 that American infants average on these tests, the average Kikuyu mental score was 108, and their average motor score, 129. *The Kikuyu infants bettered the standard score on 38 mental-scale items and on 20 motor-test items.* They were lower than the standard on only seven of the mental-test items and two of the motor-test items. However, the researchers were under the impression that these items involved implements that are familiar to American infants but not familiar to Kikuyus. When Kikuyu infant test scores month-by-month were compared with month-by-month scores for white infants in the United States and the United Kingdom, and black infants in the United States, the Kikuyu infants performed better on both mental and motor tests throughout the 15-month period of observation than did any of these other groups. However, the superiority of their performance tapered off somewhat toward the end of the period. *A number of reports have suggested that subequatorial African infants are precocious in their motor development and possibly also in their mental development, and this study appears to confirm these reports.*[10] (Emphasis added).

The mental and physical precocity of Afrikan children is duplicated by Afrikan children in America and across the diaspora. After reviewing numerous studies Jackson and Jackson (1978) conclude that "overall, the greatest precocity has been found in black infants, both in Africa and in the United States, followed by Indian infants in Latin America and infants in Asia. Caucasian infants rate lowest on the precocity scale." (Bayley (1965)[11] compared the psychomotor development of 1409 infants between 1 month and 15 months, in 12 cities across widely scattered areas of the United States. She found that Black children showed higher value for every month at every level except 15 months when compared with their White counterparts. Walters (1967)[12] compared the psychomotor development of Black and White infants across socioeconomic groups and found the Black infants to be generally superior to the White infants. It is important that we note that Geber (1958) and other observers of Afrikan infants (Bayley, 1965; Falade, 1955)[13] found that Afrikan infants were two or three months advanced over European standards in language, problem solving, and personal-social development.

Geber (1958) further concluded from her studies of Afrikan children that:

[their] ...precocity was not only in motor development: it was found in intellectual development also. It is not always realized that intellectual development is displayed very clearly in the use of the Gesell material. To take an elementary example, the child who merely looks at the cubes and then picks them up

is demonstrating a series of intellectual processes and for the building of a tower with the cubes, more complex processes are needed, in addition to the greater manual dexterity... Although most of the African children had never seen anything resembling the test material, they used it in the same way as European children and succeeded in the tests earlier than those children. Their interest was lively, and their personal-social relations excellent. They made very good contact with the tester, turning and "talking"..., smiling..., and trying in every way to communicate... .

Thus, it is undoubtedly clear that the Afrikan child, whether in Afrika, the Americas, the Caribbean or elsewhere, is very amply prepared by nature to respond adaptively to the intellectual, sociopsychological, physical and behavioral demands of his environment. Obviously, if he or she is appropriately stimulated, motivated, guided, and supported, he or she is perfectly capable of attaining intellectual heights equal or superior to the children of any other ethnic group. It is with the appropriate stimulation, motivation, guidance and support where the promise or the problem of the intellectual, behavioral, social and general personality development of the Black child lies. The "natural head start" of Afrikan children, is too often thwarted, stagnated, negated, or reversed by the inappropriateness or inadequateness of these seminal factors.

That is, the "natural head start" of many, if not most, Black children is not continued beyond early childhood for the following reasons:

- The cumulative effects of unstimulating mother/infant interactions.
- The cumulative effects of extremely young maternal age on children's intellectual development.
- The cumulative effects of the poor quality of the home environment. There is substantial evidence that the quality of the home environment of 6 to 12 month-old

children is very significantly, positively or negatively, correlated with their IQ at ages 3 and 4 (Bee, et al., 1982; Bradley and Caldwell, 1976, 1980; Caldwell and Bradley, 1978).[14]

- The cumulative effects of inadequate language and vocabulary-mastery experiences. Carew [1980] has shown that intellectual development [IQ] at three years of age is strongly related to language-mastery experiences during the second year of life.[15] Dickson and associates (1979) demonstrated that a mother's communication skills assessed when her child was 4 years old was strongly correlated with the child's IQ at age 6.[16]

- The cumulative effects of inappropriate educational and schooling experiences.

The factors just listed combine with others to produce an impoverished environment which distort, inhibit, negate, "under-actualize", the remarkable intellectual potential of Afrikan children. While such an impoverished environment may be reflective of segregated, isolated, poverty-stricken communities it may also, in fact more accurately, be reflective of impoverished psychological relations between parent, school, community, nation, and child. Children living under such impoverished circumstances tend to score far below average on standardized "intelligence" and other tests, and their IQs actually tend to decrease with age (Shaffer, 1985). Based on these tendencies, Klineberg (1963) has proposed a *cumulative deficit "hypothesis"* or theory which asserts that impoverished environments generate effects which accumulate over time and inhibit intellectual growth and functionality in children exposed to those environments. The longer children are retained in impoverished, inadequate, or inappropriate intellectual environments, the more they tend to underperform on IQ tests and underachieve in school (Jensen, 1977).[17]

Notes

1. Pearce, J. (1980) *Magical Child: Rediscovering Nature's Plan for Our Children.* New York: Bantam Books. pp. 30.

2. Sigman, M. , Cohen, S., Beckwith, B. and Topinka, C. (1986). *Task Persistence in Two-Year Olds in Relation to Subsequent Attentiveness and Intelligence.* Paper presented at International Conference on Infant Studies, Los Angeles.

3. Infant I.Q. tests Found to Predict Scores in School. *The New York Times*, Tuesday, April 4, pp. C1 and C8.

4. Individual Differences in Infants' Information Processing: Reliability, Stability, and Prediction. *Child Development*, 59, pp. 1177-1197.

5. How Infant and Mother Jointly Contribute to Developing Cognitive Competence in the Child. *Proceedings of the National Academy of Sciences*, 82, pp. 87-99.

6. Ruddy, M. & Bornstein, M. (1982). Cognitive Correlates of Infant Attention and Maternal Stimulation over the First Year of Life. *Child Development*, 53, pp. 183-188.

7. Pearce J. (1980) *Magical Child: Rediscovering Nature's Plan For Our Children.* New York: Bantam Books. pp. 42-43.

8. Ibid. 68-69.

9. Leiderman, G. (1973). African infant precocity and some social influences during the first year. *Nature* 242: pp. 247-249.

10. Jackson, F., and Jackson, J. (1978). *Infant Culture.* New York. New American Library.

11. Bayley, N. (1965). Comparisons of mental and motor test scores for ages 1-15 months by sex, birth order, race, geographic location and education of parents. *Child Development 36*, pp. 379-410.

12. Walters, C. (1967). Comparative development of Negro and White infants. *Journal of Genetic Psychology*, 110, pp. 243-251.

13. Falade, S. (1955) Le dèvèloppement psychomotor du jeune *African* originaire du Sènègal au cours de sa première annèe. Paris Foulon, cited in Geber (1965).

14. Bee, H., Barnard, K., Eyres, S., Gray, C., Hammond, M., Spietz, A., Snyder, C. & Clarke B. (1982). Prediction of IQ and language skill from perinatal status, child performance, family characteristics, and mother-infant interaction. *Child Development*, 53, pp. 1134-1156.

    Bradley, R. and Caldwell, B. (1976). Early home environment and changes in mental test performance in children from 6 to 36 months. *Developmental Psychology*, 12, pp. 93-97.

    Bradley, R. and Caldwell, B. (1980). The relation of home environment, cognitive competence, and IQ among males and females. *Child Development*, 51, pp. 1140-1148.

    Caldwell, B. and Bradley, R. (1978) *Manual for the Home Observation of the Environment*. Little Rock: University of Arkansas at Little Rock.

15. Carew, J. (1980). Experience and the Development of Intelligence in Young Children at Home and in Day Care, *Monographs of the Society for Research in Child Development*, serial no. 187.

16. Dickson, W., Mess, R., Miyake, N., and Ayuma, H. (1979). Referential communication accuracy between mother and child as a predictor or cognitive development in the United States and Japan. *Child Development*, 50, pp. 53-59.

17. Jensen, (1977). Cumulative deficit in the IQ of Blacks in the rural South. *Developmental Psychology*, 13, pp. 184-191.

Chapter 2

The Foundation of Infant Education

We have seen that the Afrikan child is born well-endowed
by nature to meet the intellectual challenges of the world.
The cognitive-behavioral potential of this child is by all
means first rate. However, potential must be actualized by
the application of appropriate educational conditions. The
education of the child begins with the education of its
parents and caregivers. Their education refers to the degree
to which they are prepared to provide the required physical,
emotional, intellectual, and social experiences and environments necessary to permit their children to acquire the
knowledge, skills, competence, qualities of personality and
character which will enable them to maintain and enhance
their lives and the life of the group to which they belong.

Traditional Afrikan social systems were sensitively aware
of the interrelatedness between the readiness for parenthood
and the stability and well-being of the society as a whole;
that poor parental preparation and unreadiness presages
familial and societal instability and vulnerability. This is
the reason the age and circumstances under which childbearing took place was strictly regulated by law and mores.
Through initiation into womanhood and manhood, a lengthy
process of education for adulthood and parenthood, traditional Afrikan society made certain that its children would
be reared in ways compatible with group integrity, survival,
maintenance of the highest quality of life as they perceived

it, and the protection and advancement of group interests. Marriage and childbearing were permitted only after completion of training and initiation. In this way, the parents and adults who reared children, did so on the basis of and in accordance with consistent, shared values, perspectives, and social goals. These traditional societies are noted for their coherence, cohesiveness and stability.

The Afrikan American community cannot maximize its existence and quality of life unless and until it educates its parents, caregivers, and those who school its children, along lines appropriate to optimizing their mental and physical potential as well as their Afrikan consciousness, identity and common humanity. A significant part of the social chaos so typical of American society, in general, can be blamed on the fact that there is little, if any, formal parenting education, that is, preparation for full adulthood and responsibility.

The revolutionary change in the education of Afrikan children must begin with changes in the parent-child caretaker-infant relationship, followed by changes in the pre-school, elementary, secondary and post-secondary and school environments.

Maternal Attitude and Fetal Development

Obviously, the nature of the physical and social relations between caretaker and infant is fundamental to the infant's development. While it is beyond the scope of this book to detail the types of physical and social interactions which will maximize the child's overall human potential, we will mention those areas of interaction which are most likely to enhance the child's positive possibilities.

Ideally, the child should be wanted and conceived for positive and psychologically healthy reasons. There is mounting evidence that a mother's attitudes and feelings about her pregnancy can influence her unborn child's personality and psychological development (Verny, 1981). Verny intimates that:

>...the unborn child is a *feeling, remembering, aware* being, and because he is, what happens to him — what happens to all of us — in the nine months between conception and birth models and shapes personality, drives and ambitions in very important ways.

An Afrikan-centered approach to parenting should emphasize to potential parents that the creation of children is a social responsibility, that their appropriate rearing and education is an adult, civic and social responsibility; that children are a gift to the community and that the most positive contribution they can make to the community and the world is the rearing of psychologically and socially wholesome children; that the having of children for psychologically and socially reactionary reasons operates against the parent's, child's and community's best interest, is counterproductive, and creates problems rather than solves them.

Physical Fitness and Child Development

The intellectual potential of the child will be optimized by a positive maternal attitude toward her pregnancy, a positive social environment, a healthy maternal body and diet. The diet consumed by the mother before conception and during pregnancy influences the child's brain and whole body development as well as its general psychological state of being (Crnic, 1983). Maternal physical fitness and diet are the means by which her attitudes toward pregnancy are conveyed to the fetus and the means by which her attitudes are expressed in physical form and to help create a physical environment which conditions the child's physical and psychological development before birth. This is especially the case where, as in the United States, mothers have pediatric and dietary options available to them if they are sufficiently motivated or enabled to take advantage of them.

The conception of a child before mother's body is physically fit can adversely affect the mental development of the child. This is the case not only for women who ingest poor diets but for women who begin childbearing too early during their life-span. In terms of intelligence as measured IQ, Record and associates (1969) have shown that as a group, the children of teenage mothers had IQs averaging 7 points lower than those of mothers who were in their middle to late twenties of comparable birth rank, family size, and socioeconomic class.[1] The number of children, especially if closely or narrowly spaced as is the tendency among Black families compared to that of Whites, can also adversely affect IQ (Record, et al., 1969; Suchindran and Linger, 1977).[2]

Prematurity, low birth weight, low weight-for-date, which are indicative of poor or inadequate maternal physical fitness and/or diet, have been demonstrated to generally negatively affect cognitive development and potential. On the whole, Black children are much more likely to be born prematurely or below weight than are White children.

Referring to his analyses of studies of relations between maternal ages, infant birth weight and IQ in Birmingham, England and Baltimore, Maryland (Record, et al., 1969; Wiener, 1970),[3] Storfer (1990) specified some findings in this area:

- The rate of premature births to Black mothers was almost two and a half times higher than among White mothers — 24.3 percent of the Black children having been born before the thirty-seventh week of gestation, compared with 10.3 percent of the White children.

- Among premature infants, the incidence of high weight-for-date babies (above 2,500 grams) was also two and a half times higher among Black families — 15.4 percent, compared with 6.4 percent among White births. Paralleling the results of the Birmingham, England study (Record,

McKeown, and Edwards, 1969b), this short-gestational-age, normal-birth-weight group had markedly lower IQs; in the Baltimore sample, their scores averaged only 88.8 (on a race-adjusted basis), compared with 95.9 for children born after thirty-eight to forty weeks of gestational period... .

- The rate of full-term but low-birth-weight infants was also markedly higher among Black families — 5.7 percent vs. 3.8 percent. The race-adjusted IQs of this group were also extremely low, averaging 92 for children weighing 2,000 to 2,500 grams at birth and 84 for children weighing less than 2,000 grams.

Marian Wright Edelman (1989) in commenting on the bleak educational, occupational and general socioeconomic future of "millions of blacks [who] today live in a desolate world where physical survival is a triumph..." noted the following:

- A black baby is almost three times as likely as a white baby to be born to a mother who has had no prenatal care at all.
- A black infant is more than twice as likely as a white infant to die during the first year of life.
- Black children in the United States face far greater health risks than white children.

She reports that in 1986:

- A black infant born in the United States was more than twice as likely to die as a white infant born that year;
- A black infant was more than twice likely as a white infant to be born at low weight;
- A black infant was far less likely than a white infant to be born to a mother who had received early prenatal care;
- A black infant was more than twice as likely as a white infant to be born to a mother who did not begin prenatal care until the last three months of pregnancy or who had no care at all.[4]

In light of the foregoing statements, we can logically conclude that the foundation for the optimal development of the Afrikan child is laid down during the pre-conceptual and prenatal periods. These periods together reflect the cultural and physical preparation of the male and female for father- and mother-hood, i.e., the appropriate timing of conception in terms of physical, psychological, and cultural maturation of the parents and the adequacy or inadequacy of appropriate medical care during the prenatal period.

The Importance of Infant Education

The first two or three years of the child's life are critical to its later intellectual, personal and social functioning. These are also the years that the brain's growth is most rapid after birth. It is also during this period that environmental experiences most effectively and fundamentally modify the brain's neurons and neuronal network. Consequently, infant education or early intervention programs, if appropriate, relatively intense, consistent, congruous and relatively long-term, can have substantial effects on the biological foundation of future learning and behavior.

Essentially, stimulation of the infant's cognitive development involves carefully interacting with and reinforcing its remarkable visual, auditory, and sensory integrative abilities. Overall, early infancy education programs are designed to help the infant: (1) achieve and maintain a state of "quiet alertness," a state conducive to learning; (2) attract the attention of the caregiver and focus his attention on the caregiver and on appropriate stimuli; (3) match visual and verbal stimuli, interesting sights and sounds; (4) learn about his body; (5) participate in educational, yet enjoyable games; (6) learn about spatial relations; (7) become highly competent at categorizing objects and sounds by learning how one object relates to another, how they are alike and different, how they differ in size, shape, color and other physical and movement characteristics; and (8) to enhance his/her self-confidence, self-esteem, sense of competence and power by using his/her body to bring about predictable changes in the world, gaining the attention and aid of others by conveying through appropriate social interaction a sense, that he/she is highly valued (Ludington-Hoe, 1987; Storfer, 1990).

In sum, the first several months of infant education involve evoking and maintaining a cognitive state conducive to learning; encouraging attentional focus, through mutual gazing, smiling, cooing, vocal imitation; creating an interesting visual, object environment; providing vestibular stimulation, physical and mental acceleration, through rocking, touching, stroking and exercising the infant's body. These activities, along with many others described and illustrated in popular and professional infant stimulation books and manuals, maintain and strengthen the infant's development of visual, auditory, manipulatory and sensory-motor coordinative competence, and early development of categorical representational competence. These competencies are all fundamental to highly positive intellectual, personal, social and socioemotional growth and functionality.

Verbal Stimulation and Intellectual Development

The infant is very competent from birth. There is evidence that infants are born with the ability to identify and reproduce 47 different *phonemes* (sounds that help establish meaning in words (Ludington-Hoe, 1987; Eimas, 1985).[5] From birth onwards the adult human voice, especially human speech, is of major importance in the development of the infant's auditory-discrimination skills and cognitive competence. Infants can make categorical distinctions between phonemes by three (3) months of age and during their first six (6) months of life. They learn to differentiate speech and language sounds from non-language and non-speech sounds, (e.g., music, bells), (Eimas, et al, 1975).[6] Infants can discriminate and respond to the pitch, variations in intensity, duration, rhythm, time and spatial patterning, and other culturally-biased speech characteristics of adult speech within their first few months of life. During the first six (6) months auditory discrimination seems to dominate over visual discrimination. There is evidence that the imitation of the infant's cooings, babblings; engaging in "vocal dialogues," vocal games, e.g., "follow the leader," "informative talk," the modeling of novel vocal patterns, naming parts of the infant's body, reading to the child on the part of the caregiver stimulate the child's auditory-discrimination development and long-term cognitive language-comprehension skills (Izard, et al, 1972[7]; Hunt, 1981[8]; Hunt, et al, 1976[9]; Hardy-Brown, et al., 1981[10]; Coates and Lewis, 1984).[11]

While it is currently not clear whether language skills precede or follow cognitive competence or how they interact with each other, it is clear that there is a substantial positive relationship between language skills, word knowledge and IQ test performance (White, 1988).

Thus, there is reason to believe that early stimulation is important to the enhanced unfolding of cognitive competence. It seems that the linguistic stimulation of the young infant during the earliest days of its life and that the language environment in which it exists fundamentally shapes its receptive and expressive linguistic, symbolic, and cognitive capacities long before it begins to speak some one-and-a-half to two (1½-2) years later. Therefore, infant education or early intervention programs which help parents to enhance the nature and quality of their social, physical and linguistic interactions with their infant, may help to maximize its intellectual, personal and social competence in face of other less conducive environmental factors.

Mother-Infant Interaction During the First Two Years — General Guidelines

After reviewing the studies of the relationship between maternal-child interactions and later IQ, Storfer (1990) concluded that:

> ...specific interactive behaviors between mothers and infants can have a considerable and seemingly lasting influence on childhood IQ scores. Behaviors of particular importance appear to include ample rocking, imitating infant's vocalizations, using gaze behavior effectively, encouraging attention to objects and events in the environment, seeking opportunities to use contingent responsivity as a teaching tool, responding immediately to an infant's or toddler's overtures and providing related ideas as part of verbal responses, and using an appropriate level of sentence complexity.

The types of maternal-infant interactions which seem to contribute to children's cognitive-behavioral development (IQ) include the following (Storfer, 1990):

1) The stimulation specifically directed *toward* the child;
2) Maternal gaze behavior patterns which are mutually pleasurable to both parties;
3) Maternal imitation of the infant's vocalizations; verbal stimulation, affective tone and informative talk;
4) Maternal encouragement of the child's focused attention on objects and events in its environment (A number of studies have found substantial relationships between infants and toddlers attention to objects and events as encouraged by their mothers and their subsequent IQ performance, particularly their verbal IQ);
5) the naming of specific objects (including the parts of the infant's body during activities such as bathing);
6) the ability of the mother to maintain the child in a state of "quiet alertness" and providing it with appropriate visual and sensory stimulation while in that state; and

7) the mother's provision of opportunities for *contingency play* or *contingent responsivity* activities on the part of the child. (Contingent play or responsivity refers to the creation of a situation which permits and encourages the infant to exercise some control over objects and events in its environment, which enables it to learn that it can consistently influence his or her surroundings through his or her self-initiated actions).

More specific suggestions and guidelines for the child's cognitive-behavioral and overall development are outlined below.

Guidelines for Enhancing Overall Cognitive-Behavioral Development

Social/Emotional Development

The social-emotional relationship between parent or caregiver and child provides the foundation on which the potency and character of cognitive-emotional behavioral intelligence is constructed. The optimal actualization and prosocial construction of cognitive-emotional-behavioral intelligence is best abetted by an emotionally warm and safe, responsive and nurturing, active and stimulating parent-child relationship and home environment. Such a relationship and environment is maximally conducive to the child's development of positive self-esteem and to his/her active, pro-active (in contrast to reactionary), prosocial learning and intellectual development. Listed below are some of the relational and teaching approaches we believe are important to the child's social-emotional development.

- Give the child a feeling of being loved and cared for by promptly and sensitively responding to its expressed physical, social and emotional needs and by allowing the spontaneous seeking and initiation of genuine social interactions with the child.

- Provide as large a quantity of "quality time" as possible for body-to-body and emotional contact through mutual touch, smiling and vocal play and talking to the child; through the gentle rocking and massaging of the infant, the eliciting and maintaining of eye contact, the encouraging stimulation of and responding to the infant's interest in the outside world.

- Respond to the child's need for adult attention and approval with verbal and non-verbal expressions of praise and support and by the appropriate setting of limits.

- Encourage the child's ability to socially and verbally express as completely as possible his/her desires and needs and to consider the consequences of his/her actions.

- Help the child to learn to accurately interpret and appropriately respond to the social behavior of the others and to his/her social environment by providing him/her with a consistent, organized, environment and emphasizing expectations that the child respect consistent, explicit, relational rules, regulations and limits on behavior.

- Respond to muted, confused or incomplete signals from the child by providing it with an accurate verbal description and explanation of its behavior and encouraging it to provide these for itself, and by modeling complete, accurate descriptions, gestural, body language, visual-facial expressions, and explanations of the parent or caregiver's own feelings and behavior.

- Encourage the child to "get in touch" with its own feelings and emotions, to appropriately identify and label expression of his emotions by permitting their "legitimate" expression, evaluation and providing guidance for their appropriate time, place and form of expression.

- Support the development of an independent, healthy sense of self and social responsibility, of self and social interest and of self-control through conversation, child-adult and doll-toy play, books, pictures and games which allow the expression and mastery of a range of feelings and emotions.
- Use stories, puppets, role play, video and audio recordings, music, proverbs and related activities to encourage the child's empathy for others and to further its moral, ethical, social sensitivity, thinking and behavior.
- Encourage the child's self-help activities, decision-making, choice-making activities by providing opportunities for such activities to occur or by taking advantage of their spontaneous occurrence.
- Provide adequate space and objects for both personal and interactive behavior.

Language and Communication Development

Gestural-behavioral, expressive, symbolic and linguistic communications both facilitate and define the essential nature of human interpersonal, social and productive interaction. The ability to effectively process and express linguistic and other symbols is inextricably and reciprocally intertwined with the formation and manifestation of cognitive, emotional, social and behavioral intelligence. The ability to receive, comprehend, process and communicate meaningful experiences, desires, needs, feelings and information evolve from and reflect the social and communicative interactions between parent or caregiver and child during the infant and preschool years. The correlation between language and/or the ability to meaningfully utilize physical, mental-behavioral signs and symbols is a strong a well-established one. Therefore, the creation

53

and maintenance of a social, linguistic symbolic and objective environment are conducive to the development of the child's intellectual and communicative competence. Language and communication experiences perhaps make the greatest contribution to brain and intellectual development. The following suggestions may be of special value for enhancing communication skills.

- Create a stable, emotionally secure and physically safe environment which provides a background which facilitates a relatively ready observation of and interaction with objects, the observation of consistent and clear human communicative and behavioral activities. The recognition of observable objects and actions of people and things lay the foundation for verbal and behavioral expression.
- Communicate with the child in a manner appropriate to his developmental level and permit him/her to express feelings, desires and needs without fear of abusive responses.
- Patiently support and encourage the child's efforts to express its desires, needs, feelings, and other experiences and the naming of its body parts and other objects and actions. Reinforce these early communicative efforts through providing an object environment where the child can engage in "hands on" activities which stimulate the general discriminative and coordinative-integrative development of the child's sensory-motor, psychomotor potential.
- Give simple one-step, well-articulated directions using eye contact and gentle touch-guidance when necessary in order to enhance listening skills and the ability of the child to direct his/her behavior according to verbal and symbolic directions. This also facilitates its learning to use language pragmatically and in the context

of ongoing activity. Gradually increase the number and complexity of steps in directions commensurate with the child's development level. One may strategically and tactfully verbally direct the child's behavior on some crucial occasions.

- Let the parent's or caregiver's as well as the child's language "map" and guide his/her behavior in the context of the chosen activity.

- Engage in immediate and reciprocal responses to the child's beginning self-initiated attempts at communication.

- Model desired behavior verbally and behaviorally for the child and support and reinforce his imitative efforts.

- Investigate and help the child gain insight into his own behavior by asking him perceptive or clarifying questions so that both he and his questioner can discover and are able to articulate and explain his needs, wants, fears and feelings.

- Acknowledge the reality of the child's perspectives, perceptions and expressed needs, desires and feelings and be careful not to invalidate them or deny their reality for the child while attempting to correct or elaborate them. Keep "mind reading" and "taking words out of the child's mouth" to a minimum.

- Encourage the child's cooperation and interactions with other children. Engage in games which facilitate his/her communicative competence.

- Pay close attention to what the child is attempting to communicate. Encourage and invite him/her to talk. Make him/her feel that his/her ideas and feelings are respected, understood and accepted and demonstrate understanding by verbally summarizing or mirroring the child's feelings and problems.

- Verbally demonstrate or model strategies by which the child may appropriately express his/her needs, desires and feelings.
- Recognize that some apparently negative behavior may signal the child's unlearned ability to express some unmet, or incompletely understood need.
- Redirect inappropriate behavior and demonstrate alternative, acceptable means for achieving the same goal of that behavior.
- Maintain consistent limits on inappropriate behavior while allowing for expression of feelings and ignore or don't over-react to inconsequential verbal behavior.
- Discuss with the child, the role, function and personal-social consequences of emotions.
- Help the child to become a good listener. Discriminative listening is very important to effective learning and behavior. Clarity and constancy of communication and direction are helpful in this regard as well as devising and playing games which stimulate good listening habits and help to develop auditory discrimination.
- Read to your child. Enhance his/her vocabulary and word power. Aid comparative and number concept development by familiarizing the child with the most descriptive words and concepts, e.g., big - little, over - under, beside - below - behind, small - smaller - smallest, same - different, more - less, etc., when he/she begins to talk or at appropriate times in language development.

Learning to Learn

Learning refers to a short-, intermediate-, or relatively long-term change in perception, ways of integrating and organizing information, of communicating, expressing and applying processed information in the world by both verbal and nonverbal means that occur as the result of experience, imitation, deliberate and/or repeated practice, and the inferential construction of concepts, procedures and rules. Because experience, models for imitation, practice, some concepts, procedures, rules of thought and behavior can be consciously manipulated and scheduled, the potency and character of learning can also, to some significant degree, be enhanced or impaired. Parents, caregivers, and "significant others" must carefully consider and influence those experiences to which the child will be exposed if they are to optimize its learning capacity.

In infancy and early childhood the proverbial "five senses" are the doors to the child's mind and the media by which his/her learning capacity is stimulated, realized, expressed and applied. Early stimulation of the senses by enhancing his awareness of his environment through planned and well designed interventions on the part of his caregivers, by enhancing the nature and quality of his/her association with his caregivers and the nature and quality of his/her reactions to and interactions with novel stimuli or novel combinations of old stimuli are crucial for the establishment of relatively advanced permanent patterns or styles of learning. These patterns or styles of learning established during infancy and early childhood have a very significant impact on the child's later learning experiences and abilities. "The child who does well has a mother or caregiver who (1) provides a rich variety of objects and toys for play, (2) allows freedom to roam and discover, (3) gives attention to her child when he finds something unusually exiting or when he encounters a problem which he cannot overcome, (4) turns everyday situations into games and (5) talks to her child" (Sparkman and Carmichael, 1973).

The foundation of positive learning rests on the provision of the social and environmental interactive experiences which stimulate the growth of the child's perceptual, and explorative and experimental as well as his/her decision-making and problem-solving competencies within a warm and supportive environment. To reinforce the child's basic learning foundation we recommend the following:

- Support the child's maturational efforts to focus on tasks, to interact with objects, people and situations through the media of all its senses.
- Encourage the child's attempts to maintain sustained attention in play, explorative, individual and group activities and to develop persistence and task completion orientation.
- Help and encourage the child's discovery and use of numerous problem-solving approaches through helping him to focus and refocus his attention, the modeling of alternative strategies and the planned rearrangement of the object and the social-relational environment.
- Demonstrate patience with the child's fledgling efforts and provide adequate time for task completion.
- Avoid or minimize frustration by matching learning tasks with the developmental level and by not driving the child beyond his/her self-determined interest, attention-span and level of endurance.
- Let the child interact with other children who can model the use of successful strategies, team learning, cooperative behavior and who can help him/her learn to conform to mutually beneficial social expectations and to learn to delay immediate gratification.
- Use hints, clues, cues and talking the child through tasks in helping him/her acquire new abilities and skills when necessary.
- Break developmental learning tasks down into manageable steps, use physical, concrete and verbal cues to direct or redirect child in task or activity completion, ask and let the child verbalize the steps of a tasks or activity and reinforce his successful efforts with

tangible rewards, praise or physical expressions of approval and administration.

- Take turns with the child in completing learning tasks.
- Provide the child with a fairly consistent schedule of play and rest activities and types and quantities of reinforcements as means of establishing regular and effective cognitive behavioral and learning patterns and styles.
- Do not move the child too rapidly from one learning task or activity to another. Allow adequate transition time, i.e., time to move smoothly between activities. Prepare the child to undertake new activities by providing him/her with a sense of "closure" or completion relative to the prior activity and by announcing far enough ahead of time that the current activity is nearing its end and that the new one is to follow. Some preliminary talking about the new activity before entering may provide the child with the "mind or mental set" conducive to productive learning experiences.
- Be aware of and make use of the child's preferred learning style, e.g., visual, auditory, touch, etc., by providing learning materials, resources and approaches appropriate to that style. However, helping the child to maximize his/her use of other styles and helping him/her to coordinate and to integrate various styles are also to be encouraged and supported.

Movement and Play Development

The infant's motoric or movement activities, i.e., the child's physical-behavioral interaction with the environment provide a platform for the construction of intelligence and the acquisition of basic knowledge. Intelligence ultimately involves the adaptive use of workable or appropriate means to achieve certain ends. This basic means-end differentiation and adaptive coordination begins in infancy with the modification the congenital reflexes and with motor or movement activities which represent adaptive responses to the environment and which both give rise to mental operations or thoughts and which are guided by these same processes. Like motor or movement activity intelligence and learning involve the foundational development of at least four categories of understanding concepts of objects, their permanence and relationships, space, time, and causality. This time period referred to as infancy or more specifically, the sensorimotor period is the period during which intelligence is constructed based on the child's increasing sensory perceptual and movement.

Play is the child's work. Through it the child comes to know and develop himself, to recognize, assess and hone his talents, skills, and abilities; comes to know nature and laws of the physical world; and comes to know the social world and how to function within it. Play involves acts of cognition-attention, concentration, imitation, repetition, exploitation, experimentation, role playing, the taking of various perspectives, imagination, abstraction, conceptualization, numbering, recalling, anticipating, communicating, practice, thinking, etc. Consequently, the ultimate potency and character of intelligence, in good part, reflect the construction and organization of the child's interactive sensory and movement space and the quality of the child's play, learning activities, games, and social relations. Following are some suggestions for supporting and enhancing the child's intellectual development through movement and play.

- Interact with the child in ways which increase his/her awareness of his/her body and its relationship to other objects in the environment through labeling and tactile interactions and through placing various objects of various types, colors, shapes, textures, sounds, within reach of the child such that he interacts with them in increasingly systematic ways.

- Provide enough objects of various types which stimulate the child to engage in gross and fine motor activities, (e.g., handling, throwing, crawling, swinging, climbing, catching, balancing, walking, running, jumping) and serve to increase the child's awareness of the organization of space, the relationship of objects among themselves and to him/herself.

- Use mobiles, age-appropriate toys, stackable, nest-able or form-fitting, interlocking objects, mazes, puzzles, objects for stringing, cutting, drawing supplies, indoor and outdoor play, to provide opportunities for the child to experience spatial relationships. This situation should also provide the caregiver with opportunities for modeling guiding the child through movement and play activities that center around the exercise and development of rhythm, balance, coordination skills.

- Provide the child with occasions to engage in a variety of tactile and small motor activities (e.g., water and sand play, pegboards, puzzles, blocks, legos, etc.)

- Encourage the child to independently select play, game and learning materials and support his/her appropriate, innovative or novel use of them.

- Encourage the child's initiation and participation in various types of play with other children (e.g., interactive, parallel, sociodramatic, etc.) and to organize its own play.

- Allow the child opportunities to lead in play with the caregiver who is responsive to his/her leadership. Model verbal and physical play with toys.

- Provide interesting walks, tours, visits and the like and utilize these as opportunities for enhancing the child's observational skills, for stimulating provoking questions designed to excite and satisfy the child's natural curiosity.

- Make reading and writing entertaining leisure and play-time activities. Encourage the child's efforts to read by sharing reading activities with the caregiver. Read to him/her from the beginning weeks of life as often as possible. Read on a regular basis; make a wide variety of printed material available; make pencil and paper readily available (curiosity regarding and interest in writing begins as an interest in scribbling and drawing); and stimulate and support the child's interest in reading, writing and general knowledge by praising his/her efforts in this regard, by touring the library, bookstores, buying books, writing stories dictated by the child him-/herself, display his/her paperwork and surround the child by a literate world.[b]

In addition to the suggestions delineated above, we think the ones made by Meyerhoff and White (1986) as outlined in the *Table 1* are especially pertinent, particularly the section which deals with "Things To Avoid."[12]

---

[b] The above recommendations were in part adopted from the booklet, *Today's Challenge: Teaching strategies for working with children prenatally exposed to drugs / alcohol.* The Los Angeles Unified School District, Division of Special Education, Pre-natally Exposed to Drugs (PED)Program, March, 1990.

Table 1
A PRIMER FOR PARENTS

The following recommendations are based on the lessons we learned from parents of linguistically, intellectually and socially competent preschool children.

THINGS TO DO

• Provide your children with maximum opportunity for exploration and investigation by making your home as safe and accessible as possible.

• Remove fragile and dangerous items from low shelves and cabinets, replace them with old magazines, pots and pans, plastic measuring cups and other suitable playthings.

• Be available to act as your children's personal consultant the majority of their waking hours. You do not have to hover, just be nearby to provide attention and support as needed.

• Respond to your children promptly and favorably as often as you can, providing appropriate enthusiasm and encouragement.

• Set limits — do not give in to unreasonable requests or permit unacceptable behavior to continue.

• Talk to children often. Make an effort to understand what they are trying to do and concentrate on what they see as important.

• Use words they understand but also add new words and related ideas. For example, if your child gives you a red ball, say, "This ball is red, just like my shirt. Your shirt is blue and it matches and it matches your pants."

• Provide new learning opportunities. Having children accompany you to the supermarket or allowing them to help you bake cookies will be more enriching than sitting them down and conducting a flashcard session.

• Give your children a chance to direct some of your shared activities from time to time.

• Try to help your children be as spontaneous emotionally as your own behavior patterns will allow.

• Encourage your children to pretend activities, especially those in which they act out adult roles.

THINGS TO AVOID

• Don't confine your children regularly for long periods.

• Don't allow them to concentrate their energies on you so much that independent exploration and investigation are excluded.

• Don't ignore attention-getting devices to the point where children have to throw a tantrum to gain your interest.

- Don't worry that your children won't love you if you say "no" on occasion.
- Don't try to win all the arguments, particularly during the second half of the second year when most children are passing through a normal period of negativism.
- Don't try to prevent your children from cluttering the house — it's a sure sign of a healthy and curious baby.
- Don't be overprotective.
- Don't bore your child if you can avoid it.
- Don't worry about when your children learn to count or say the alphabet.
- Don't worry if they are slow to talk, as long as they seem to understand more and more language as time goes by.
- Don't try to force toilet training. It will be easier by the time they are 2.
- Don't spoil your children, giving them the notion that the world was made just for them.

Notes

1. Record, R., McKeown, T. and Edwards, J. (1968). The Relation of Measured Intelligence to Birth Weight and Duration of Gestation. *Annals of Human Genetics*, 33, pp. 70-79.

2. Suchindran, C., & Linger, J. (1977). On comparison of birth interval distribution. *Journal of Biosocial Science*, 9, pp. 25-31.

3. Record, et al., 1969; Wiener, 1970; Wiener, G. (1970). The Relationship of Birth Weight and Length of Gestation to Intellectual Development at Ages 8 to 10 Years. *Journal of Pediatrics*, 76, pp. 694-699.

4. Edelman, M. (1989). *Black Children in America 1989*. N.Y.: National Urban League Inc., p. 63.

5. Eimas, P. D. (1985). Perception of Speech in Early Infancy. *Scientific American, 252*, No.1, pp. 15-16.

6. Eimas, P., Sigueland, E., Jusczyk, P., and Vigorito, J. (1971) Speech Perception in Infants. *Science, 171*, pp. 303-306.

7. Izard, B., Cooperman, O., Joseph, A., and Izard, J. (1972). Environmental effects on language development: a study on young children in long-stay residential nurseries. *Child Development,* 43, pp. 337-358.

8. Hunt, J. MCV (1981). Experiential roots of intention, initiative, and trust. In H.I. Day (ed), *Advances in Intrinsic Motivation and Esthetics.* N.Y.: Plenum.

9. Hunt, J. MCV., Mohandessi, K., Ghiedssi, M, and Akiyama, M. (1976). The psychological development of orphanage-reared children: Intervention and outcomes (Tehran). *Genetic Psychology Monographs, 94,* pp. 177-226.

10. Hardy-Brown, K., Plomin, R., and DeFries, J., (1981). Genetic and environmental influences on the rate of communicative development in the first five years of life. *Developmental Psychology, 17,* pp. 704-717.

11. Coates, D., and Lewis, M. (1984). Early mother-infant interaction and infant cognitive status as predictors of school performance and cognitive behavior in six-year-olds. *Child Development, 55,* pp. 1219-1230.

12. Meyerhoff & White, B. (1986). Making the Grade as Parents. *Psychology Today, 20,* No. 9, September, pp.38-45.

Chapter 3

Educational Practices
in Toddlerhood

The quality of the home environment during infancy (during the first two years) in terms of the mother's emotional and verbal responsivity to the child; her use of restriction and punishment in controlling the child's behavior; organization of the child's physical environment, and of the time she spends with the child around various indoor and outdoor activities; her provision and interactive use of appropriate play materials with the child; involvement with the child and the opportunities she provides for daily stimulating the child in a variety of ways, has been shown to be substantially correlated with the child's IQ at ages three and four (Bradley and Caldwell, 1976[1]; Bee, et al., 1982[2]).

In fact, Bradley and Caldwell (1976) and Bee and associates (1982) found that the quality of the home environment when children were 6 or 12 months-old had a significantly higher correlation with their IQs at 3 and 4 years old than did their performance on infant "intelligence" tests. In addition, Yeates and colleagues (1983[3]), found that the quality of the home environment during infancy and early childhood was a better predictor of children's IQs at 4 years old than was the IQ of their mothers (as measured before the children's birth).

The appropriate use of various educational toys and books by mothers to stimulate their children has been shown to very markedly enhance IQ and academic performance of the children (Levenstein, 1970). However, two crucial factors which interact with and reinforce all of the activities taking place in the home environment and which have been shown to enhance the child's intellectual development is the quality of the mother's linguistic interaction with the child and/or her encouragement of the child's linguistic advancement. Carew (1980)[4] concludes, from studies observing interactions between caretakers and their children, that language-stimulating activities particularly in conjunction with other specific educational activities and interactions between caretakers and children during their second year are strongly related to the overall intellectual development and moreover, language development, of the children at three years of age. Shaffer (1985) aptly sums up the discussion at this juncture when he states that:

> ...an intellectually stimulating home environment is one in which parents are warm, responsive, and eager to the involved with their child. They describe new objects, concepts, and experiences clearly and accurately, and they provide the child with a variety of play materials that are appropriate for her age and developmental level. They encourage the child to ask questions, to solve problems, and to think about what she is learning... When you stop and think about it, it is not at all surprising that children from these "enriched" home settings often have very high IQs; after all, their parents are obviously concerned about their cognitive development and have spent several years encouraging them to acquire new information and to practice many of the cognitive skills that are measured on intelligence tests.

Researchers who have studied highly gifted and eminent populations (Fowler, 1925, 1983; Cox, 1926; McCurdy, 1957; Bloom, 1982a, 1982b) have generally concluded that intense parent-child interaction is regularly associated with intellectual precocity. These caretakers generally demonstrated unusual attention to the child's intellectual development; engaged in frequent early stimulation; applied intensive educational measures; and provided a high quality early home education.

Toddler Education

We have seen that mother-infant interactive behavior, in particular mother-initiated linguistic interactive experiences during the first two years of the infant's life, is strongly correlated with preschool intellectual competence. Around age two to two-and-a-half (2-2½) interactive language — mastery experiences in conjunction with behavior control techniques (e.g., restrictiveness, punitiveness, independence, spatial organization and play materials and experiences) appear to be strongly correlated with cognitive and language development and competence during the early childhood as well as the primary school years (Storfer, 1990).

A number of longitudinal studies indicate that how effectively caregivers exercise discipline and control of children during toddlerhood have a substantial influence on IQ scores and academic performance in early childhood and in adolescence (Barnard, et al., 1984[5]; Caldwell & Bradley, 1984[6]; Bradley & Caldwell, 1984[7]; McCall, et al., 1973).[8] On the whole, behavior control techniques which appear to be the most effective in maintaining and enhancing their cognitive competence include: (1) clarity of rules, regulations, policy and behavioral requirements; (2) consistent reinforcement of those rules and policy so that children can predict the consequences of misbehavior or of positive behavior; (3) punishment which provides the opportunity to instruct and make available to the child alternative behaviors which are rewarding; (4) punishment which is administered promptly after an infraction of policy, that is firm but not harsh, that is "fair" and executed as a penalty for infraction of rules, not as an expression of parental anger, frustration, displaced aggression and other personal problems having little to do with the child's behavior; (5) when a relatively high (but not overly restrictive) degree of control is exercised in a family atmosphere of love, warmth, cohesiveness, genuine emotional and behavioral expressiveness, a reasonable degree of initiative and independence among members, positive moral-spiritual attitudes, relatively low intra-familial conflict, and a tangible sense of respect for family values, learning and skills development.

In a series of studies Jean Carew (1980) found that intellectual experiences initiated and structured by parents in conjunction with the child and other caregivers are strongly predictive of high-level cognitive competence when they include opportunities for language, spatial, perceptual, fine motor, and expressive artistic skills mastery, as well as when they provide stimuli for evoking and supporting concrete reasoning and problem-solving behavior during the second year of life. During its third and fourth years the child appears intellectually to benefit most from (1) language-mastery experiences generated by solitary and interactive situations; and (2) spatial-mastery experience (multisensory integrative — i.e., experiences which utilize games and toys to stimulate and develop general movement, discriminative movement, auditory, hand, graphic, logical, and social thinking (Furth & Wachs, 1975).[9] Maxwell (1985)[10] suggests specific ideas for enhancing children's intellectual and social functioning between the ages of two and three years. They include teaching the child (a) to share; (b) human relations; (c) manners; (d) neatness; and (d) treating the child as a learner and a mathematician; and (f) exposing the child to scientific puzzles, to a multicultural nursery and to a wide variety of games; as well as to have story, music and happy time.

In this section we have presented evidence that demonstrates that the quality of parental interaction with infants and toddlers, the intellectual, social, emotional, physical, recreational/educational environment they create for their children are substantially correlated with the children's later cognitive development.

Families generally create and maintain social and intellectual environments which can accelerate, maintain, or impair the intellectual and social achievement of their children. Differences in social and intellectual environments maintained by families occur not only across socioeconomic classes but within classes as well. For example, Clark (1983) found fairly distinct differences in the family environments of poor Black families whose children were academic high achievers and poor Black families whose children were academic low achievers. A list of the comparative differences are outlined in *Table 2*.

Marjoribanks (1972) provided an interesting series of studies which measured the interrelationships between mental ability test scores (Verbal, Number, Spatial, and Reasoning) and scores of the home environments of Black and White children across social class. The home environment was measured in terms of the degree to which it emphasized intellectually stimulating activities and provided or availed the children to intellectually supportive material and cultural resources both inside and outside the home. Marjoribanks (1972) noted that "there is a cultural difference between [Blacks and Whites] in the home experience in parent-child interactions, even within the same economic stratum, that may help to explain the different intelligence test performance by members of the two cultures." Some of the major differences between the two groups included their relatively higher or lower: intellectual expectations and aspirations; level of knowledge regarding the development of their children; rewards for accomplishments; emphasis on language usage; provisions for enlargening vocabulary; emphasis on correct language, parents language usage; provisions for home learning, for outside learning, learning supplies (books, etc.) and the provision of learning assistance to their children. The home environmental factors

Table 2[c]

A Comparison of the Quality of Success-producing
Patterns in Homes of High Achievers and Low Achievers

	HIGH ACHIEVERS	LOW ACHIEVERS
1	Frequent school contact initiated by parent	Infrequent school contact initiated by parent
2	Child has some stimulating, supportive school teachers	Child has had no stimulating, supportive school teachers
3	Parents psychologically and emotionally calm with child	Parents in psychological and emotional upheaval with child
4	Students psychologically and emotionally calm with parents	Students less psychologically and emotionally calm with parents
5	Parents expect to play major role in child's schooling	Parents have lower expectations of playing role in child's schooling
6	Parent expect child to play major role in child's schooling	Parents have lower expectation of child's role in child's schooling
7	Parents expect child to get post-secondary training	Parents have lower expectation that child will get post-secondary training
8	Parents have explicit achievement-centered rules and norms	Parents have less explicit achievement-centered rules and norms
9	Students show long-term acceptance of norms as legitimate	Students have less long-term acceptance of norms

[c] Clark, R. (1983). *Family Life and School Achievement: Why Poor Black Children Succeed or Fail.* Chicago: University of Chicago Press.

71

	High Achievers	Low Achievers
10	Parents establish clear, specific role boundaries and status structure with parents as dominant authority	Parents established more blurred role boundaries and status structures
11	Siblings interact as organized sub-group	Siblings are less structured, interactive subgroup
12	Conflict between family members is infrequent	Conflict between some family members is frequent
13	Parents frequently engage in deliberate achievement-training activities	Parents seldom engage in deliberate achievement-training activities
14	Parents frequently engage in implicit achievement-training activities	Parents less frequently engage in implicit-achievement training activities
15	Parents exercise firm, consistent monitoring and rules enforcement	Parents have inconsistent standards and exercise less monitoring of the child's time and space
16	Parents provide liberal nurturance and support	Parents are less liberal with nurturance and support
17	Parents defer to child's knowledge in intellectual matters	Parents do not defer to child in intellectual matters

which Marjoribanks found to be the most influentially interrelated with children's mental abilities are included in *Table 3*. Apparently, appropriate applications of the five home environmental variables listed there among other related factors can measurably help to maintain or increase the child's intellectual, academic and social achievement.

Table 3

Home Environment Emphases Most Influentially
Related to Children's Mental Ability Scores†

HOME ENVIRONMENT EMPHASIS		CHARACTERISTICS
Educational and Social Achievement	1a.	Level of parental expectations for child's education.
	1b.	Training in prosocial behavior and human relations.
	1c.	The aspirational level of child's parents.
	1d.	Amount of preparation and planning for child's education.
	1e.	Level of accuracy of parents knowledge of child's educational progress.
	1f.	Level to which educational accomplishments are valued.
	1g.	Intensity of parental interest in school.
Activeness	2a.	Extent, variety and intellectual, personal-social growth content of indoor activities.
	2b.	Extent, variety and intellectual, personal-social growth content of outdoor activities.
	2c.	Extent and the purpose of the use of the TV and other media.
Intellectual Development	3a.	Number and variety of thought-provoking activities engaged in by children
	3b.	Opportunities made available for thought provoking discussions and thinking.
	3c.	Use of books, periodicals, and other literature (in home and libraries).
Development of Independence	4a.	Freedom and encouragement to explore the environment and solve own problems.
	4b.	Stress on early independence.
Language Usage	5a.	Language (standard English use and reinforcement).
	5b.	Opportunities available for language usage, the development of "word power" and vocabulary.

† Adapted from Table 1, of Marjoribanks, K. Race and IQ, and the Middle Class. *Journal of Psychology* vol.69, 1977 No. 3 pp. 266-273
Trotman, F. (1977) Race, IQ and the Middle Class. *Journal of Psychology* vol.69, 1977 No. 3, pp. 1015-1025

Parent Training for Cognitive Development

The foregoing discussion implies that if certain parent-infant interactions are related to enhanced intellectual functioning during and after childhood, then teaching parents more effective methods of interacting with their infants might be effective in preventing cognitive deficits or in enhancing their children's intellectual capacity. There is substantial evidence that teaching parents to engage in effective infant-education can be successful (Drash & Stotberg, 1972, 1979: Klaus & Gray, 1968, Weikart, 1968; Fowler & Swenson, 1979; Gordon 1969, Levenstein, 1969; Metzl, 1980; White 1981, 1985, 1988).

This evidence makes the case for the immense importance of home-based interventions for maintaining and enhancing the intellectual potential of Afrikan children. Home-based interventions refer to interventions that take place in the home before and during pregnancy or rather early in the child's life (soon after birth and/or during the first three years) which are designed to systematically involve the parents and other family members in the child's learning experiences. The early start is recommended since the foundation for intellectual growth and the basic structure of the personality is essentially completed by three years of age. During this period most parents hold high hopes for their infants. This optimistic outlook in conjunction with the fact that this is also the period of the most rapid intellectual and physical growth for the child, and is the period when primary life-long influential emotional relationships are established, provide the seminal condition for maximizing the child's human potential. A home-intervention program can be most successful not only when it educates both parent and child, but also when it is coupled with the upgrading of parental academic, personal-social, and occupational skills. The enhancement of parental self-esteem, self-acceptance, cultural pride and identity, are

74

important factors in transforming the social-emotional and intellectual environment of the home.

A remarkable example of the level of intellectual gain that can be had by parent training or *home-based intervention* programs is the one executed by Levenstein (1970).[11] Utilizing books and toys conceptualized as "verbal interaction stimulus materials" Levenstein's research team worked with disadvantaged 2-year-olds and their mothers in order to promote the cognitive growth of the children. The central vehicle for promoting that growth was the development of intellectually stimulating verbal interactions between mother and child by demonstrating to the mother how the materials could be used to stimulate the child. Their use was demonstrated to the mother in the home during half-hour visits twice per week over a 7-month period. As described by Levenstein the research team or "toy demonstrators" modeled how and encouraged mothers to stimulate verbally-oriented play between themselves and their children. The toys and books and the parent child. The toys and books and the parent-child interactions centered around them "were the focus of eight kinds of verbal-stimulation techniques." The demonstrators taught the parents to focus the child's attention and learning on *verbal categorization* and:

1. Gave information (labels, form, color, size, etc.).
2. Described her own toy manipulation (building, matching, etc.).
3. Elicited responses (questions, etc.).
4. Verbalized social interaction (invited, directed, etc.).
5. Encouraged reflection (alternatives, consequences, etc.).
6. Encouraged divergence (alternatives, consequences, etc.).
7. Engaged interest in books (fostering "representational competence" by eliciting verbalization about illustration, etc.)

8. Gave positive reenforcement (verbal support, helping, etc.).

The experimental group (the parents and children who received demonstration training) in contrast with a matching or control group of parents and children who did not participate in the training, received an average of 32 visits and were left with a total of 28 books and toys to be utilized in mother-child interactions. Average IQ gains of 17 points were attained by the children who took part in the program during the seven months that the program was in effect. The control or non-participating group of children showed no changes in IQ during the same period. Follow-up evaluations found that the participating group of children were still outperforming their non-participating counterparts on measures of IQ and academic achievement in the fourth, fifth, and sixth grades (Lazar & Darlington, 1982)[12]

An added benefit of Levenstein's program was that the younger siblings of the participants were often intellectually and psychologically enriched as well. This additional benefit along with the fact that the participants showed *long term* gains in IQ and academic achievement, seems indicative of the strong possibility that the home-based intervention prepared the parents to become more competent at stimulating the intellectual development of their families in general and to provide an intellectually stimulating home environment long after the formal demonstrations and training ended.

Genevieve Painter's (1969) work with ten culturally disadvantaged children provides another example how a well-designed home-intervention program can maintain and enhance children's preschool intellectual performance. Painter's ten racially mixed children were exposed to a one-hour-a-day, five-days-a-week training program which emphasized language development, symbolic thinking and representation, concept formation, and fine-motor development. These children attained an average IQ of 108.1, some 15.1 points higher than their elder siblings who had attended traditional nursery schools.

Finally, Garber and Heber (1973) enlisted forty children at ages three to four months from the most poverty-stricken areas of Milwaukee, Wisconsin in an intense infant and early childhood education program. The combination home- and center-based program presented a curriculum which emphasized cognitive and social development until age six and which also provided a successful maternal rehabilitation component, produced children who attained IQ scores averaging 121 (on Stanford-Binet) at the end of their education, compared with 87 for their control counterparts.

For the reader who would like to implement some of the suggestions we have made at this point and who would like well-illustrated, informative, detailed sources to aid them in their practice, please see the *Appendices*. This list consists of mass publications and is by no means exhaustive. Reader discretion is advised in implementing any of the approaches the authors may recommend.

Notes

1. Bradley, R. & Caldwell, B. (1980). The relation of home environment, cognitive competence, and IQ among males and females. *Child Development*, 51, pp. 1140-1148.

2. Bee, H., Bernard, K., Eyres, S., Gray, C., Hammond, M., Spietz, A., Snyder, C., and Clark, B. (1982). Prediction of IQ and language skill from perinatal status, child performance, family characteristics, and mother-infant interaction. *Child Development*, 53, pp. 1134-1156.

3. Yeates, K., McPhee, D., Campbell, F., and Ramey, C. (1983). Maternal IQ and home environment as determinants of early childhood intellectual competence; A developmental analysis. *Developmental Psychology*, 19, pp. 731-739.

4. Carew, J. (1980). Experience and the development of intelligence in young children at home and in day care. *Monographs of the Society for Research in Child Development*, serial no. 187.

5. Barnard, K. Bee, H., and Hammond, M. (1984). Home Environment and Cognitive Development in a healthy low-risk sample: The Seattle Study. In A.W. Gottfried (ed.), *Home Environment and Early Cognitive Development*. Orlando. Florida: Academic Press.

6. Caldwell, B., & Bradley, R. (1984). *Home Observation for Measurement of the Environment, Administrative Manual*. Little Rock: University of Arkansas Press.

7. Bradley, R. & Caldwell, B. (1984). 174 Children: A study of the relationship between home environment and cognitive development during the first 5 years. In W. Gottfried (ed.), *Home Environment and Early Cognitive Relationship Development*. Orlando, Florida: Academic Press.

8. McCall, R., Appelbaum, M., & Hogarty, P. (1973). Developmental Changes in Mental Development. *Monographs of the Society for Research in Child Development, 38,* serial no. 150

9. Furth, H., & Wachs, H., (1975). *Thinking Goes To School*, New York: Oxford University Press.

10. Maxwell, W. & Maxwell, M. (1985). *52 Ways to Raise the IQ of a Child*. Pearland, Texas: The IQ Foundation.

11. Madden, J., Levenstein, P. & Levenstein, S. (1976). Longitudinal IQ outcomes of the mother-child program. *Child Development*, 47, pp. 1015-1025.

12. Lazar, I. & Darlington, R. (1982). Lasting effects of early education: A report from the Consortium for Longitudinal Studies. *Monographs of the Society for Research in Child Development*, 47, (2-3, Serial No. 195).

Chapter 4

Preschool Education

We have seen that the quality of the social relations between parent and infant and the quality of the home environment during its first three years of life have a major impact on the socioemotional and intellectual growth and development of the child. However, if the child's social and intellectual growth is to be continuous then it must be further stimulated and reinforced by social and learning experiences fostered by institutions outside the home environment. Prior to the entry of the child into elementary school, preschool programs and institutions may be designed to fulfill such experiential roles.

Since the 1960s, a number of preschool educational research programs have been implemented which have manipulated the quality and content of the educational environment of Afrikan American children with the objective of maintaining and increasing their intellectual performance. These programs and research projects were based on the hypothetical assumption that with appropriate stimulation the ability of children and adults to succeed academically could be significantly improved. There were a number of variations in preschool experimental design. Some, as discussed above, involved home-based interventions; others involved center-based interventions, where the children were exposed to a variety of educative procedures in learning centers outside their homes; still other programs involved a combination of home-based and center-based interventions. While such programs have not been equally successful in enhancing the intellectual potential of their target populations, it can be stated that they have been generally successful and some have proved to be outstanding. On the whole, well-implemented experimental preschool programs fully warrant the conclusion that children can profit very significantly from various preschool curricula which provide a wide range of specific experiences that stimulate the child's growth and development of linguistic and cognitive competence, good personal, educational and social habits.

As Weikart and Lambie (1970) contend, the primary role of the preschool curriculum is:

> (1) to focus the energy of the teacher on a systematic effort to help the individual child to learn, (2) *to provide a rational and integrated base for deciding which activities to include and which to omit,* and (3) to provide criteria for others to judge program effectiveness so that the teacher may be adequately supervised. The successful curriculum is one that permits this structuring of the *teacher* to guide her in the task of interaction with the theory she is applying, on the one hand, and the actual behavior of the child, on the other. (Emphasis added)

The scope of this book will not allow us to review in any detail the number of successful preschool programs which have been undertaken during the past thirty years. Moreover, we will be unable to discuss the relative merits of these programs. Our purpose herein is to substantiate the assertion that preschool programs can enhance the social and intellectual development of children; that the creative application of a curriculum rationally related to the developmental psychology, (i.e., biological and personal-cultural assets) of children and rationally related to their future goals and responsibilities can successfully boost their intellectual power and social competence. We will briefly summarize some of preschool programs which have been successful in the enhancing cognitive competence of preschool children in terms of IQ measurements and a number of social outcome evaluations.

Bereiter-Engelmann Academic Preschool Program

The objectives of the Bereiter-Engelmann Preschool program (Bereiter and Engelmann, 1966) were strongly cognitive in orientation and included the teaching of language, reading and arithmetic to preschool "disadvantaged" children. Specific learning objectives and instructional approaches were devised and students were exposed to structured curricula areas based on task analyses, well-defined concepts, operational procedures and predetermined, intensive, sequential drills. Evaluations by Bereiter and Engelmann and others (McDill et al., 1969; Beller, 1973; Miller and Bissell, 1983) indicate that the program produced substantially higher IQ scores and academic scores in academic areas such as arithmetic.

Gordon's Parent Education Program

Gordon and his colleagues (1969) designed and executed a program of parental education which began when the children of poor Afrikan American families in northern Florida were three months old, and continued until the children were three years old. The intent of the program was that of enhancing the mother's self-esteem and "normalizing" or increasing the children's cognitive and personal development. Gordon's program included the training of paraprofessionals to demonstrate specifically designed home learning activities to each mother once per week, and to assist the mother in teaching the child. At age 2 the children were enlisted in a backyard "home learning center" where "parent-educators" (paraprofessionals) worked with five children and one mother based on a Piagetian curriculum which emphasized the learning of concepts appropriate to the children's level of intellectual and psychological development. This program permitted maternal involvement in the home learning center and also provided the parents with education counseling, education, and parenting training. At age 1 Gordon's experimental children proved superior

in cognitive development relative to their control counterparts. Between the ages of 3-3½ years they attained IQ
scores between 91 and 116. At age 4 the experimental group
scored significantly higher on a variety cognitive measures
than the control group. The cognitive gains tended to be
larger for those children who participated longer in the
program (Stallings and Stipek 1986).

The Syracuse Preschool Project

Lally (1973) of Syracuse University instituted a preschool
program referred to as the Family Development Intervention
Program which was designed to augment the intellectual
and social development of a group of parents and their
children from low socioeconomic backgrounds. These families
also suffered from a number of social as well as economic
problems.

Lally's program consisted of a number of training and
educational components; (1) a prenatal and early infancy
program beginning as early as three to six months before
the birth of the children and at six months of age up to age
two. During this period the mothers were provided with
information and advice on prenatal and child nutrition,
techniques for promoting the child's development, and given
counsel regarding ways of coping with family problems. The
paraprofessionals who provided these services also encouraged the mothers to use routine child-care activities as
opportunities for instituting positive social-emotional
interactions with the child, for creating and sustaining the
child's language experiences, sense of competence and for
the construction of his or her positive self-concepts. The in-
home program was supplemented by a half-day center-based
program at six months which expanded to a full-day multi-
age center-based program by age two.

The center allowed the children free choice among games
designed to stimulate small- and large-muscle exercises,
expressive play, listening and looking activities, etc.,

supervised by different teachers in different areas of the center. Weekly, in-service training sessions were held for the center's staff and parents who wanted to attend. Frequent interactions between parents and staff members were emphasized and encouraged.

At age 3, a group of children exposed to Lally's program attained an average IQ score of 111. An average IQ score of 111.0 was attained by another group of thirty-seven children at age four. A subgroup of experimental children (children who participated in the program) outperformed their control counterparts (children who did not participate in the program) on IQ tests by an average of 13.4 points.

The Montessori Method

This system originally designed to teach retarded and poor Italian children has been demonstrated to provide a viable approach to the education of Afrikan American children (Miller and Bissell, 1983). The method focuses on three major developmental areas: motor, sensory, and language education. Motor activity is considered essential for mental development and many specific exercises and activities have been designed to stimulate fine and large-muscle coordination and skills development. Sensory development is stimulated and maintained by the use of elaborate materials of a large variety of shapes, sizes, colors, weights, smells, etc. Language education follows specific guidelines for teaching children to name objects, recognize concepts, and pronounce words and at age 4, academic learning — writing, reading and arithmetic. Miller and Bissell (1983) and others (Stalling & Stipek, 1986) have demonstrated that the Montessori method can produce long lasting and relatively high levels of academic and cognitive achievements by children who have been exposed to the program. This is apparently in good part due to the fact that Montessori method achieves a good match between the children's cognitive capacity and the educational materials utilized by the program, and the individually paced self-correcting choices made by the children in interaction with their teachers (who are more accurately described as resource persons and facilitators assisting the children to advance to the next phase of the program).

The High/Scope Perry Preschool Program

This program is of particular interest here because it has been subjected to detailed, long-term follow-up evaluations across a relatively wide range of intellectual and social variables. The High/Scope preschool curriculum evolved from the Ypsilanti-Perry Preschool Project, a carefully structured program designed especially for the enrichment of disadvantaged children who are educationally retarded (Weikart, 1979). Mechinger (1984) describes the target population of the study in the following way:

> In brief the project focussed on 123 black children from poor families. Children with IQ's from 60 to 90 were selected and then randomly divided into an experimental group, which was offered high-quality pre-school education at the age of 3, and a control group without that advantage. Fewer than one in five of the parents had completed high school. Forty-seven percent of the children lived in single-parent homes.

In the monograph, *Changed Lives,* (Berrueta-Clement et al., 1984) the High/Scope program is outlined and its effects on youths from age 3 through 19 are analyzed. The effects of the program on its participant's school, early socio-economic success, and social responsibility are presented and thoroughly discussed.

The High/Scope program is essentially a cognitive/developmental curriculum rationalized in accord with Piagetian theory (Schweinhart et al., 1986). It is an "open" school model in which the teacher and preschooler work together in planning, initiating and executing the pupil's learning activities. The program seeks to engage the children in developmentally appropriate educational experiences in order to develop the child's ability and skills in a number of areas including the arts, physical movement; conceptual thinking; language arts (speech, drama, communication, graphic representation); social relations (working with others); decision making; time and energy planning and management; and the application of acquired reasoning skills to a broad range of academic, practical, natural situations and a variety of material and circumstances (National Diffusion Network, 1986). The children are encouraged to achieve beyond their original plan in the areas of cognitive, social, and emotional development through planning — doing — reviewing with the support of their teachers their learning activities. Parents were encouraged to be involved in the program through home visits on a weekly basis by members of the staff. The children attended classes in half-day sessions, 5 days per week over the entire school year. After 2 years of preschool, the experiential group attained significantly higher IQ ratings than did their control counterparts. At age 14, the treatment group scored significantly higher than the control group on several tests of academic achievement.

Mechinger (1984) summarized the overall results of the High/Scope program as follows:

Black children who 16 years ago at the age of 3 benefitted from preschool education have grown up with markedly greater success in school and in their personal lives than a comparable group without early childhood education, according to a landmark research project in Michigan.

Compared with another group of children in the study who did not receive the early education, more of the preschool children, who are now 19 years old, graduated from high school and are employed. Fewer have been in trouble with the law or had teenage pregnancies....

Now, at age 19, their record shows that the rates of employment and participation in college or vocational training after high school group were nearly double those of youths without preschool education; teen-age pregnancies in the group were slightly more than half those among the non-preschool girls; preschool graduates were involved in 20 percent fewer arrests and detentions; nearly 20 percent fewer had dropped out of high [school]....

Sixty-seven percent of the preschool group had graduated from high school at the age of 19, in contrast to 49 percent of the control group. For those who went on to form of academic or vocational study after graduation, the difference was 38 and 21 percent.

High/Scope's accomplishments give pertinent testimony to the influential impact early childhood education can have on adult behavior.

Project Head Start

Project Head Start is probably the most visible and best known preschool compensatory intervention program designed and implemented to enrich the cognitive and social development of disadvantaged children. Initiated as a summer program in 1965 as "the first national intervention effort for preschoolers" (Natriello, et al., 1990), Head Start now provides two years of preschool instruction and services for its participants. According to Natriello and his colleagues (1990), Head Start was commissioned by the Office of Economic Opportunity to provide child development services including the following:

- Enhancement of the child's intellectual and academic skills
- Improvement of the child's physical health
- Improvement of the child's socioemotional development
- Involvement of the family in the child's development
- Improvement of the family's functioning as a social unit

In a more general sense, Shaffer (1985) states that:

...the goal of Head Start (and similar programs) was to provide disadvantaged children with the kinds of educational experiences that middle-class youngsters were presumably getting in their homes and nursery school classrooms. It was hoped that these early interventions would compensate for the disadvantages that these children may have already experienced and place them on a roughly equal footing with their middle-class age mates by the time they entered first grade.

A comprehensive evaluation and critique of Head Start programs since its inception by CSR, Inc., of Washington, D.C., generally concluded that overall, the intervention programs had statistically significant and positive effects on the cognitive and socioemotional development of children. That is, they generally improved the "short term" thinking and academic skills, self-esteem, social behavior, achievement motivation and relatively longer-term effects on the physical health, motor development, and nutrition of the children.

Evaluation of long-term follow-ups of a number of (11) early intervention programs by Lazar and Darlington (1982)[1] and Collins (1983)[2] concluded [as reported by Shaffer, 1985] that children who participated in early intervention programs compared with the intervention nonparticipants from similar social backgrounds demonstrated (1) immediate gains on IQ tests and other measures of cognitive development; (2) higher scores on tests of reading, language, and mathematics achievement; (3) a greater ability to meet their school's basic requirements (i.e., less likely to be assigned to special education classes to be retained in grade or to drop out of high school); and (4) enhanced positive attitudes toward achievement in school and job related activities.

Finally, the early intervention programs seem to have had positive effects on maternal attitudes as indicated by their greater satisfaction with their children's academic performance. The mothers of the participants held higher occupational aspirations for their children compared to the parents of nonparticipants.

After reviewing and discussing the implications of a collaborative study of fourteen early intervention programs, Lazar (1980) concluded that "any well-designed, professionally supervised program designed to stimulate and socialize infants and young children from poor minority families will be efficacious."[3] McDill and colleagues [in Natriello, et al. 1990] indicate that those preschool programs show the most promise which demonstrate the following characteristics: (1) meticulous planning and lucidly stated objectives; (2) high ratio of instructional staff to students; (3) instructional objectives that are closely tied to program objectives; (4) high intensity of treatment; and (5) rigorous training of instructional personnel in the methods and content of the program.

It should be kept in mind that preschool programs vary widely in design, pedagogical approach and philosophy. Consequently, such programs vary widely in their impact on their participants' cognitive and social development. Thus, evaluations which combine several differing programs without noting important differences (sometimes subtle but very important) among them, may appear to indicate a general failure of early intervention programs to significantly and positively influence their participants' cognitive abilities. However, as pointed out by Bronfenbrenner (1974),[4] it generally is the programs that employ traditional nursery school approaches which fail to show much cumulative effect of intervention on the cognitive and academic skills of disadvantaged children. He further intimates that those programs which employ structured curricula demonstrate greater success in improving the cognitive development of their participants. Levine and Havighurst (1989) commenting on Bronfenbrenner's review of research concerning early intervention programs noted the following:

Since Bronfenbrenner's review of research on early intervention, even more encouraging results have been reported concerning the effects of outstanding preschool programs to enhance the cognitive development of low-status students. In general, these data suggest the low-status students who have participated in cognitively oriented preschool programs do substantially better in school than do children of comparable background who did not participate.

The Marcus Garvey School — An Afrikan-centered Curriculum

The Marcus Garvey School, founded in 1975 by Dr. Alvin Palmer, in Los Angeles, California, is perhaps the best example to date of the Afrikan-centered schools, programs, and curricula to boost the intellectual, academic and social achievement of Afrikan American children beyond that attained by other alternative educational programs. Afrikan-centered programs base their curricula and pedagogical approaches on the past and contemporary sociohistorical, sociocultural experiences and future goals of Afrikan peoples the world over; on the developmental psychology and characteristics of Afrikan children and adolescents; and on the development in Black students of an operationally stable and enduring Afrikan identity and consciousness.

Award-winning Marcus Garvey School which enrolls children from two years old through ninth-grade, emphasizes academics in its preschool as well as elementary grade, and junior high school programs. The effectiveness of its Afrikan-centered approach can be appreciated by our citation of a few of the many remarkable demonstrations by Garvey students which have been noted in many publications.

- Two-year-olds learn to recite their alphabets in English, Swahili and Spanish.
- Three-year-olds can recite the Latin names of all the major bones in the body and can recognize all fifty

states on a map, can name all the states and cite their capitals with minimal assistance of their teachers.

- It is commonplace for four-year-old pre-schoolers to read from third through sixth grade books. In fact, Garvey students are usually three or more grade levels above their national grade average in reading and mathematics.

- At Garvey, algebra is taught in fourth grade and trigonometry and calculus taught in the early grades.

- Garvey third grade students scored higher on both reading and math than sixth graders from a public school for gifted (predominantly White children) on identical tests administered to both classes.

The unusual achievements by Marcus Garvey School are not based an the exclusive admissions policy nor on the higher education credentials of its teaching staff. According to its founder, "We take any Afrikan child and just start building." Most of the teaching staff does not have a college degree as a matter of school policy. Garvey School success seems to be based on its Afrikan cultural perspective, Afrikan-based school culture, its emphasis on providing an Afrikan historical context for all classes and studies, on the development of Afrikan identity and consciousness, the development of a positive self-image and pride through the intense study of Afrikan and Afrikan American history, individualized attention, and allowing each student to progress at his or her own pace. Moreover, no more than fifteen students are assigned to each teacher and close parental involvement in maintaining high student motivation and dealing with discipline problems make very significant contributions to the schools success record. Additionally, culturally-aware teachers hold and express high expectations of their students and who sincerely believe in their students' ability to learn. Teachers are free to initiate, create and innovate in the classroom where the students are taught to deal with real life problems and situations and to believe in themselves.

Interim Summary and Conclusion

Our review of early intervention programs indicates that substantial long-term increases in IQ, substantially enhanced academic and social functioning can be induced in children by immersing them in enriched, socially positive, responsive and cognitively stimulating preschool home and institutional environments. This is especially the case if parents have been prepared to act as the primary agents of intervention in the home during the children's first three years. Their intervention begins with the provision of appropriate prenatal and postnatal medical attention and nutrition; the provision of an emotionally warm and emotionally responsive relationship with the children. Parents should be trained, counseled and supported in order to avoid being overly restrictive and punitive toward their children; to provide them with a safe, organized, economically secure physical environment; consistent age-related recreational and learning activities; age-appropriate play materials, toys and playful interactions between parent and child which maintain the child's interest, attention, alertness, curiosity, experimentation; on-going parental involvement with the child; and (the providing of) opportunities for introducing variety in the child's daily life.

It is beyond the scope of this book to provide specific, detailed, practical methods of infant education. A sizable number of lay and professional books and journals are readily available which provide this type of information. Our major objective herein is to impress the reader with the fact that "intelligence can be learned," can be nurtured. In fact, intelligence which is not nurtured, shaped, supported by and is unresponsive to interactive experiences with the worlds of things, peoples, feelings, challenges, ideas, and the like, is without meaning and is of little real value. Intelligence, its continual actualization throughout the life-span, and its effective application to the life problems of the individual, of the people, and of humankind, must be cultivated and attended to with care and sensitivity.

The cultivation of intelligence begins before conception. The procreation of children should be entered into with the utmost consideration and respect for their future, not for the reactionary, self-centered, short-sighted, negative emotional satisfactions of their parents. These attitudes may become potent influences, for better of worse, on both the pre-natal and post-natal development of the offspring.

The pre-natal environment, both internally and externally, i.e., inside the mother's womb and outside in the mother's social world, should be as healthy and nurturing as possible. Maternal stress and neglect is fetal stress and neglect; maternal insecurity, fetal insecurity. These negate and/or bias infantile intellect and personality. Therefore, it is imperative that society make a first priority of protecting and maintaining the physical and emotional viability of its families and children. No social and economic reality, ideology, or practice should be allowed to rationalize and justify the neglect of children; to condone their use and abuse for the selfish and venal purposes of others. A well-nourished mother and child residing in a socioemotionally supportive environment provides the foundation for optimal intellectual, emotional, social, moral, and spiritual develop-ment of the child, and ultimately of the people.

Notes

1. Lazar, I & Darlington, R. (1982). Lasting Effects of Early Education: A Report from the Consortium for Longitudinal Studies. *Monographs of the Society for Research in Child Development, 47*, (2-3, Serial No. 195).

2. Collins, R. (1983, Summer). Head Start: An update on program effects. *Newsletter of the Society for Research in Child Development*, pp. 1-2.

3. Lazar, I. (1983). Discussion of the implications of the findings. In Consortation for Longitudinal Studies (ed.), *As the Tree is Bent... Lasting Effects of the School Programs*. Hillsdale, N.J.: Lawrence Erlbaum. pp. 461-466.

4. Bronfenbrenner, U. (1974). Is Early Intervention Effective? A report on longitudinal evaluation of preschool programs. DHEW No. (OHD)74-25. Washington, D.C.: U.S. Department of Health, Education and Welfare. pp. 273, 286, 305.

Chapter 5

Afrikan Children and
Afrocentric Society

Children are born into social systems, societies. They are
an integral part of a full social system for they are its
beneficiaries and grow up to become its benefactors — or
malefactors. Therefore, children are not merely born into
a family or are the mere products of their parents' procre-
ative efforts. They are born into a society. They are gifts
to society. Nurtured by their family and society, they can
represent that family's greatest gift to their social world.
Therefore, the conception, bearing, birthing and rearing of
children — the educating and training of children to have
a sense of social responsibility and purpose, social and
cultural identity, high and healthy self-regard and respect
for others, are of key importance in the development of a
truly wholesome community or society.

Children conceived as a result of ego-centric, self-centered,
reactionary, anti-social needs and drives; children who are
reared as mere by-products of parental and societal emotional irrationalities, without a sense of social responsibility
and belongingness; without a parental and societal sense
of cultural consciousness, values, purposes, will become
children and adults who will on the whole produce a society
teetering on the precipice of regression; who experience an
unnecessarily low-quality of life, lives of self-destruction,
and who will be vulnerable to negative peer- pressure or
social conditions. Intelligent children maximize their own
survival. But their personal survival can only be maximized
within a secure and creatively intelligent sociocultural

system. Outside a wholesome social system personal "intelligence" is without meaning. In fact, without such a system, truly intelligent children — i.e., children who become socially productive adults, adults who together resolve social-cultural problems of survival and who work to enhance social-cultural quality of life — cannot be predictably and abundantly produced.

With this in mind, we must recognize that the production of "truly intelligent" Afrikan children requires the existence of a very stable, yet dynamically creative, pervasive Afrikan-centered consciousness in the Afrikan community. For this consciousness forms the maternal and social matrix, the womb out of which beneficently intelligent Afrikan children and nations are born. This Afrikan-centered matrix structures, supports, nurtures and provides meaning and purpose for Afrikan intelligence. Beneficent Afrikan intelligence cannot be nurtured in a cultural vacuum or in cultural confusion. Therefore, it is of vital importance that the nurturers of Afrikan children — mothers, fathers, and/or other caregivers and caretakers — be assimilated into Afrikan culture and values.

If, in an Afrikan-centered cultural context, Afrikan children are conceived, carried in the womb, born, reared and educated with a feeling of being loved and cared for; helped to develop specific mental and physical skills at appropriate periods of their development; encouraged to take interest in the outside world; provided with appropriately stimulating language, motor-sensory, problem-solving environments and experiences, with caretakers who design and supervise a safe, intellectually positive socioemotionally stimulating world for them, caretakers who act as both benevolent authorities and consultants for them, who foster coping skills, social competence, self-acceptance, -esteem, -confidence, -love, and social interest — then their overall needs, intellectual and otherwise, will be satisfied.

Afrikanizing Infant Education

While we support the concept of infant education, we must warn the reader that such an undertaking must be executed with consummate sensitivity, appropriateness and respect for the infant's limitations, comforts and interests. The infant should not be forced, overwhelmed, or pushed to the point of frustration. Education should be a recreational, playful, joyful, exciting experience for the child. And the child should be allowed to signal its beginning and termination. Forced teaching will only teach the child to associate learning with negative emotions and feelings, and, moreover, may lead him/her to reject or resist new learning experiences. It is very important that intellectual growth not be overemphasized and that the child be stimulated and educated holistically, i.e., in terms of all developmental areas (intellectual, social, physical, personal).

Furthermore, while we recommend that parents and professionals take advantage of numerous books, journals, articles, manuals, and programs which provide guidance for executing infant education and early intervention programs, we must also indicate that such programs are not "race-neutral." That is, while the sensory/motor exercises, types of equipment, motives, and many play/educational toys and objects are "race-neutral," the context in which they are utilized and sociocultural and personal purposes they are designed to serve may not be. The absence of Afrikan-American dolls, games, books, etc., may subtly help to alienate the child from its ethnic and cultural roots and identity. The child's room and home should reflect a love for Afrocentric culture e.g., filled with Afrikan pictures, sculptures, picture books, music, and the like. Afrikan-centered cultural events, occasions, celebrations, rituals — enjoyable outings in the company of warm, harmonious Afrikan adults — provide the all-important sociocultural, socioemotional and sociointellectual context for the growing infant.

Mass-market infant education programs are based on Eurocentric culture and are ultimately designed to serve Eurocentric sociocultural interests, a number of which are inimical to Afrikan liberation and prosperity. While the current infant education programs may maintain or accelerate the Afrikan child's intellectual potential when executed outside of an Afrikan-centered cultural context, his/her intellectual growth and character may be alienated from their Afrikan origins. If such intellectual alienation continues into adulthood the benefits of its intellectual potential will be lost to Afrikan culture and peoples. In fact, in a number of important instances, such alienated Afrikans may unwittingly be used to ally themselves with Eurocentric forces against Afrocentric interests.

It is also important to remember that, as discussed earlier, the rate and growth of the *psycho*motor abilities of Afrikan children generally are significantly more advanced compared to those of European children. Mass-market and professional infant and early childhood education programs are based on psychomotor developmental and growth averages of White children. This information implies that expectations regarding the Afrikan child's ability to equal and surpass the programmatic milestones established by the infant/early education projects should at no time be lowered or doubted. As we also earlier intimated, the Afrikan child has a *natural* "head start." The principal function of Afrikan infant/early childhood education is to maintain and enhance that "head start" and to protect its integrity from the corrosive effects of White racism and imperialism.

Social Environment and Intelligence

Infant and early childhood education and intellectual preparation need not require that the parent be formally or highly educated or that he/she provide the infant/child with highly structured, formalistic, didactic educational exercises and experiences. Expensive toys, elaborate equipment, inordinate amounts of time utilized developing learning instruments and arranging the child's learning environment are not necessary. Interpersonal games, parent attention and creative, stimulating, social interaction, genuine love and sensitive care, a wholesome physical social and psychological home environment — are the most potent stimulators of children's intellectual, personal and social development. A realistic desire on the part of the child's caretakers that the child shall actualize its human potential to the fullest extent possible; the holding of reasonably high expectations for the child's intellectual, personal and social potential; a creative use of not only the home environment, but of the sociocultural environment and facilities outside the home to stimulate and support the child's overall development, are also potent instruments for furthering its intellectual growth.

The large majority of children have prospered intellectually and otherwise without being subjected to formal, home-based education programs. These children profited from having grown up in social environments which inculcated in them the personality characteristics which facilitated their learning processes under more formal and school-like circumstances. These characteristics can be instilled in children whose parents have relatively little or no formal education or who, for whatever reason, cannot provide their children with a formal infant educational program. If children can be encouraged to develop the following characteristics by whatever wholesome means parents have at their disposal then their ability to do well in school and life will be assured:

- Ability to attain and maintain attentional focus
- Ability to listen discriminately
- Ability to utilize language effectively both receptively and expressively

- Ability to maintain positive, social interactions and relations
- Ability to observe carefully and discriminately
- Ability to maintain self-control and adequately cope with frustration

The child should exhibit a reasonable or high degree of:

Respect for adults
Independence
Persistence
Curiosity
Experimentation
Exploration
Discovery
Moral/ethical standards
Universal sense of justice
Respect for order
Punctuality
Neatness
Cleanliness
Respect for property
Responsibility

Social interest
Good manners
Etiquette and social grace
Sensitivity to persons and environment
Self-esteem/family and community pride
Commitment to promises made or contracts
Love of learning
Ethnic/cultural identity
General care for humans of all races
Reverence for life.

Self-concept and Self-esteem:
Expanding and Assimilating the Afrikan Self

The sense of a subjective self (me) and non-self (it, they), the foundation of personal identity begins early in life, perhaps as early as 3-6 months of age if not earlier (Mahler, Pine & Bergman, 1975).[1] Certainly, by the end of their second year some children are already utilizing the personal pronouns *I, me, my, mine* when referring to themselves and *you* when speaking to one another (Shaffer, 1985).

Shaffer (1985) further indicates that:

This linguistic distinction between I and you suggests that 2-year-olds now have a firm concept of "self" and "others" (who

99

are recognized as selves) and have inferred from their conversations that *I* means the person (or self) who is speaking whereas *you* refers to whomever is spoken to.

Between their first and fifth years children can classify themselves and others according to social categories (e.g., stranger, familiar, age — "child," "adult," "big boy," "little boy," ...; gender — male, female). Between ages 3½ and 5 children begin to acquire the concept of a private, thinking self. By or around age 3 Afrikan American children are conscious of some ethnic differences e.g., "White" vs non-white or "Black" (Clark & Clark, 1958).[2] Thus, it is apparent that the foundation of personal identity, of self-perception, and of self-evaluation begin construction very early in life. These "self" factors fundamentally shape and direct other related "selves" or personality factors and through their mediation, shape and direct behavior of all types throughout the rest of the individual's life.

Social experience, that is, the nature and quality of social interactions the child has with other people, the group(s) to which he/she belongs, are some of the most important determinants of his/her personal identity. The child looks at reflections of himself cast by a "social mirror." We can infer from this information that the type and quality of social experience provided by a child's caretakers is of crucial importance in how the child (and adult) will perceive and evaluate him- or herself. The individual's self-perception and evaluation markedly influence his intellectual as well as his personal and social behavior.

Shaffer (1985) defines self-perception or self-concept, and self-evaluation or self-esteem as follows:

Self-concept: one's sense of oneself as a separate individual who possesses a unique set of characteristics.
Self-esteem: a person's feelings about the qualities and characteristics that make up his or her self-concept.

It must be kept in mind that while the definitions of "self-concept" and "self-esteem" emphasize uniqueness of the self in contrast to other selves, this does not mean that one's self-concept does not contain important characteristics held in common with others — characteristics whose evaluations help to determine self-esteem. Ethnicity is one (among others) of those personal characteristics one shares with many others. Consequently, how a person responds to his/her ethnicity (within a particular societal context) has a very potent effect on self-perception and self-evaluation.

Significant negative self-perception and relatively low self-esteem have been found to be factors in emotional mental ill-health, psychosomatic symptoms, drug abuse, personal and interpersonal incompetence, social maladjustment, academic under-achievement, low vocational aspirations and initiative, and juvenile delinquency (Rice, 1987).[3]

An individual can exhibit relatively high self-esteem because he has a broad, positive self-concept or because he has negated unacceptable aspects of his self-concept through various forms of psychological suppression, denial and distortion and can therefore only consciously perceive the constricted, though positive aspects of his self-concept as representing the whole of who he is. The individual's self-concept and related self-esteem, whether generally positive or negative, may be founded on a relatively large or very restricted number of perceived personal characteristics. The latter part of the prior statement implies that an individual can unconsciously or unknowingly harbor negative perceptions about important aspects of himself and still "feel very good" about who he thinks he is. Good feelings about oneself can be based on ignorance of reality and of oneself (i.e., lack of self-knowledge; false consciousness).

The foregoing discussion implies that as concepts, self-concept and self-esteem, are not monolithic, indivisible ideas. A self-concept may be not only negative or positive, but broad or restricted, conscious and unconscious, realistic and/or unrealistic. Self-esteem may be based of a rather broad spectrum of the individual's self-perceived characteristics or a relatively small — sometimes one — number of characteristics. It is quite possible for the individual to consciously note certain incompetencies, inadequacies, and impairments in his personality and yet feel quite good about himself if he perceives these factors as not important to his self-definition, social acceptance and standing or paradoxically, perceives their existence as enhancing his self-definition or social status.

Susan Harter (1982)[4] developed a concept (and scale) of self-concept which includes four factors — cognitive, social, physical competence, and general self-worth. Given this multi-dimensional conception of the self-concept, it is theoretically possible that a person may exhibit relatively low cognitive competence and yet feel very good about himself. It is possible that a person's high self-esteem may be almost exclusively based on a high physical competence (e.g., great athletic talent) or social competence (e.g., high social popularity, lots of friends) compared to relative incompetence in the other three areas.

Interestingly, high competence in certain areas, e.g., cognitive or academic competence, may not translate into significantly higher feelings of self-esteem by the person who exhibits it. In fact, in some instances the expression of a high level of competence or ability by some individuals may be a source of negative self-esteem. For example, Rice (1987) noted that:

> Boys from minority groups are less likely to develop a positive self-concept from high achievement. Rosenberg (1965) found that these boys as a group had distinctly lower grades than other boys and *not necessarily low self-esteem*. About one-fourth who had better-than-average grades had higher self-esteem — not because of their grades but in spite of them *for high grades were criticized by this minority group.* (Emphasis added)

The Social Bases of Self-Esteem

A survey of 3,000 children from various ethnic groups commissioned by the American Association of University Women,[5] found that while a majority of White schoolgirls suffered a heavy loss of self-esteem between third grade and high school... "Far more Black girls surveyed were still self-confident in high school compared to White and Hispanic girls, and Whites lost their self-assurance earlier than Hispanic girls" (Daly, 1991). The latter citations imply that Afrikan American girls may base their self-esteem on some different factors than do European American girls.

Self-esteem also seems to be related to social context. For instance, Rosenberg and Simmons (1972) found Black adolescents who attend White schools evidence a lower self-esteem than Black students who attend predominantly Black schools; Black students who attend segregated schools have a higher self-esteem than Black students who attend integrated schools; overall ... "Black youths have higher self-esteem when not exposed to White prejudices" (Rice, 1985).

Apparently, some Black youths may base their self-concept and self-esteem more on social and other factors than on school performance. Daley (1991), from her review of self-esteem in the Black and White schoolgirls, concluded:

>...the answers that Blacks gave regarding their relationship with teachers prompted the researchers to conclude that black girls draw their apparent self-confidence from their families and communities rather than the school system... .

One of the researchers cited by Daley suggested that "in order to maintain that self-esteem [Black girls] are dissociating from school." Many Afrikan American families seem to have been remarkably successful in maintaining the self-esteem of their children in the face of pervasive racism and economic hardship. However, this success might, in some instances, have been achieved through the unnecessary sacrifice of higher intellectual and academic achievement on the part of many Afrikan American boys and girls. This very likely possibility requires us to examine more closely the concept of self-concept relative to Black children.

An individual's self-concept can be his source of self-esteem and simultaneously, can be inadequate for resolving important problems of living confronting him and his social group. Simply because a person is happy with his self-concept does not mean that that self-concept is adequate, appropriate, or efficient in the face of certain current and future problems. This is especially true when the self-concept of the individual has been constricted so as to avoid, to escape, and/or deny that important problems, problems perhaps threatening to his very survival, even exist — a self-concept constructed or designed to delete certain troublesome aspects of reality. This type of constricted self-concept may be in part inherited by the individual from the culture of his social group. Because the constructed self-concept "shuts out" unpleasant reality and motivates the individual to perhaps pursue more immediate gratification, hedonistic pleasures, escape responsibility, permits him to engage in self-aggrandizing and palliative fantasies, charades, fads, and other types of retreats from reality, he may feel relatively secure and happy with this constricted view of himself.

White racism and imperialism poses serious, difficult challenges and in many instances, life-threatening problems for Blacks. White imperialistic and racist propaganda undermines the self-confidence of Blacks in their full humanity, intelligence, creativity — their innate capacity to develop a civilization superior to that of Europeans through the use of their god-given abilities. Because Afrikan Americans and Afrikans have allowed Eurocentric dis-information campaigns to convince them that science, mathematics, technology, and general academic excellence are not originally and inherently "Afrikan," and can be independently comprehended and applied by people with black skin equally as well or superior to any other people — many Afrikan Americans and Afrikans have refused to include high level cognitive or intellectual competence in their definition of themselves or their self-concept or their concept of what it means to be Black or Afrikan. They have been duped into thinking that to pursue intellectual excellence is to pursue a "white" prerogative; is to "act white," to pursue a hopeless dream since "niggers don't know nothing about math and science anyway," "only nerds and squares want to read all the time," "reading and learning ain't going to do you no good anyway, 'cause the whites ain't gonna let you get equal with them". "Reading and math in boring, what good is learning this going to do me?" "None of my other friends do any homework. Why should I?" "I don't want everybody thinking I am some kind of freak reading all the time." "Music and basketball, that's where the money is". They have resigned themselves to servitude and second-class status because they have lost their faith in their ability to triumph over White domination or because they are too afraid to try. For them the source of all their troubles and perceived inabilities is their blackness, their skin, their Afrikanness — not the result of pathological White racism. Consequently, they infer from this fallacious belief that, if they exclude from their self-definition the pursuit of knowledge and intellectual excellence — if they don't try to "act white" (*read:* pursue knowledge and independent political/economic power); if they can deny and hide as much as possible their blackness, their Afrikanness — then they will be happy. Thus is born what we shall refer to as an *alienated self-concept.*

The individual of Afrikan descent, who may be designated as demonstrating an alienated self-concept, is one who exhibits the following characteristics:

- He has unconsciously, and often consciously, accepted White racist stereotypes of Afrikan and Black people as fact.

- He may reactionarily define himself in a way which permits him to reject his Afrikan identity (both the real and the stereotypical) and to assume an alien, or non-Afrikan or neutered identity, or a diffuse, unstable, contradictory identity.

- He may reactionarily identify with White racist stereotypes of Blacks with a vengeance in a failed attempt to negate his stereotypical identity by exaggerating it.

- He builds his identity almost exclusively on extrinsic or external factors, e.g., the types of people he associates with, the exhibition of status symbols, the adoption of fads, "in-group" mannerisms, dress codes and styles, the pursuit of social popularity, the practice and expression of anti-social behavior and attitudes.

- He is essentially self-centered, short-sighted, superficial, avoidant, and individualistic to a fault — having a limited sense of social responsibility, social interest, or of social priorities as far as Afrikan people are concerned.

- He mainly is motivated by seeking self-aggrandizing solutions to his problems, by treating and relieving his symptoms rather than solving the problems which are the causes of his distress.

- He has little confidence in his capacity to truly be the equal of other men. He may feel that such is not his destiny. Consequently, even when he may possess unsurpassed intelligence or talent, he may feel that he can only achieve full and ultimate recognition when placed in the service of his White oppressors.

- In sum, he has refused to pursue and gain true self-knowledge of his Afrikan heritage, and has failed to integrate his true ethnicity into his self-concept and personality.

The individual of Afrikan descent who may be designated as demonstrating a *wholistic self-concept*, is one who exhibits the following characteristics:

- He has consciously and unconsciously rejected White racist stereotypes of Afrikan people as fact.
- He does not reactionarily define himself but proactively defines himself in terms of his Afrikan culture, heritage and reality, and in terms of the reality of his personal and social experiences and expectations. Thus he defines himself in ways which permits him to assume an authentic, coherent, cohesive Afrikan and human identity.
- He builds his identity on both intrinsic and extrinsic factors; on his association with Afrikan-centered persons and those who respect his Afrikanness; on consumption and cultural symbolic displays which uplift him and his people and maintain their mental and physical health and welfare; on pro-social behavior and dress.
- He develops and appropriately transforms his attitudes, associations, perceptions, ways of defining himself and the world which permit him to directly comprehend and confront reality and to take personal responsibility for helping to rectify his, and his people's problems as well as problems common to humankind.
- He is "centered," balanced between a wholesome drive for self-preservation and continuing positive evolution and a wholesome drive for group preservation and evolution. His love for self and group are synonymous and he maintains a healthy sense of social interest, responsibility, and priorities. He recognizes that his personal health and powers are finally dependent on the health and power of his ethnic group. The priorities

of his ethnic group come first. He is dedicated to the liberation of his people from bondage of all types.

- He is motivated by his self-determined needs based on accurate, realistic, self-examination; self-knowledge and self-acceptance; on self-actualization, task-oriented problem-solving drives to resolve conflicts which bedevil him and his ethnic group.
- He is realistically self-confident. He does not doubt his capacity nor that of his people to equal or surpass the accomplishments of others. He feels that his talents are best displayed and utilized in the service of his people and against domination by other people.
- He realizes knowledge of truth and the continuing, joyous pursuit of knowledge are liberating. He is deeply aware that Afrikan peoples have the longest scholarly and intellectual tradition, that scholarship and intellection are Afrikan traditions and inherently Afrikan. When he practices mathematics, science, philosophy, etc., he celebrates the best of Afrikan tradition and through such practices maintains Afrikan cultural identity and consciousness. He recognizes that there is nothing foreign or alien about his pursuit of the highest level of cognitive competence of which he is capable.
- He avidly seeks self-knowledge, knowledge of his and other cultural groups; knowledge of the world and of reality in general. He seeks to be productive and contributive. He continues to integrate into his personality and self-concept an honest knowledge and sense of ethnicity. The infrastructure of his personal and social identities consist of a resolute and unassailable sense of ethnic pride, ethnic and human connectedness.

The *wholistic self-concept* is a broad, well-rounded type of self-perception. It is based on the acceptance and appropriate transformation of reality and not on escape, avoidance, and defensive distortion of reality as in the case of persons demonstrating the alienated self-concept. For the reality that the alienated Afrikan person denies and distorts, avoids and escapes, is the reality which contains an important number of potentially marvelous and healthy human potentials — intellectual, social, emotional, spiritual, ethical-moral, material-economic possibilities. By cutting himself off from important aspects of reality — from challenging opportunities for growth experiences and the development of useful skills — the alienated Afrikan person cuts himself off from alternative solutions to his problems, alternative sources of person-social pleasure and satisfaction and self-actualization.

The *alienated self-concept*, though it may be utilized to help make the person feel good about himself, may still be deemed inadequate because such a concept does not include the need to develop and utilize in the best interest of oneself and one's social group, certain valuable personal, social, and intellectual talents and competencies. The lack of or underdevelopment of these skills and competencies — or if developed their misdirected employment — (e.g., using them to support one's oppressors) leads to or maintains both on a personal and group-wide basis poverty, dependency, socioeconomic subordination, self-negating and self-defeating behavior.

Therefore, it is socially and culturally imperative that the alienated, self-serving self-concept which characterizes too many of Afrikan Americans be broadened and deepened if the quality of Afrikan life is to be enhanced and Afrikan liberation and continuing survival be assured. In this context, that means that Afrikan American children be encouraged and conditioned to develop a wholistic self-concept which includes perceiving themselves as intellectually and humanistically the equals of children of other ethnic groups. They must be motivated to base important aspects of their self-esteem on the full development and appropriate personal and social use of their intellectual and related socio-personal talents. The development of a wholistic self-concept in Afrikan children may be aided by the following recommendations.

- Intellectual and academic excellence should be more intensely publicly acclaimed, highly honored and rewarded in modern Afrikan culture.

- Information concerned with the intellectual, social, cultural accomplishments and contributions of Afrikan peoples, nations, and individuals should be widely disseminated in the Afrikan community and learned by each succeeding generation of children.

- The accomplishments of Afrikan peoples and cultures, heroes and heroines, important cultural transitions (both positive and holocaustic), should be celebrated and commemorated.

- Afrikan homes and social institutions should present a tangible Afrikan cultural presence and facade.

- Afrikan holidays, feast days, festivals, ritual ceremonies, initiation rites, dress customs should be increased and celebrated more intensely.

- Afrikan children should receive an Afrikan-centered cultural and academic education.

- An intellectually-stimulating environment should prevail in Afrikan homes, communities and institutions.

- Intellectually-gifted Afrikan children should be positively reinforced for their efforts, supported and protected from injurious social forces and negative peer groups.

- High expectations regarding academic performance and social responsibility should be evidenced by parents and educational personnel.

- High quality infant and childhood education of Afrikan children should be supported and expanded so that intellectually and socially useful competencies can be solidly developed early in life so they may become the sources of personal pride and important elements in construction of positive self-concepts.

- School culture should be organized and regulated so that expensive personal adornments — such as faddish, gaudy instruments and gadgets, expensive sneakers, jackets and other clothing, cosmetics and other luxury items — do not become the primary sources of students' self-esteem, social status, popularity, obsessive attention; sources of student envy, jealousy cliques, dissension, conflict, and possible violence. School uniforms or firmly enforced restrictions on the items just listed would be in order. This would be done in order that students need to gain distinguished social status will be satisfied in terms of academic pursuits and accomplishments or their excelling in other culturally positive activities and displays of their talents and abilities.

- Afrikan children should receive more effective moral/ethical thinking skills training and be encouraged in their development of a healthy spirituality.

Psychologist, Darlene Powell-Hopson (1987) has presented evidence which indicates that concerted educational efforts in the home and schools can improve Afrikan children's ethnic pride and help them to develop a more wholistic self-concept. She has suggested a special curriculum and recommended training for parents which can be utilized to bolster Black children's self-perception and self-esteem (Powell-Hopson, 1990) Janice Hale-Benson (1986) also makes pertinent suggestions and recommendations in this regard, particularly with reference to improving the cognitive-intellectual development of Black children.

Summary

Our cursory review of successful early educational intervention programs clearly indicates that substantial and long-
lasting increases in measured intelligence can be obtained
by children who, based on their family's "cultural disadvantages," would be expected to suffer from "cumulative
deficits" in their learning abilities and motivational
orientations. Generally, these programs may include the
education, training and/or supportive counseling of parents
or other caregivers regarding effective child development
principles, milestones, abilities and educational/
recreational/socioemotional procedures which can be utilized
to maintain or enhance the cognitive-social development
of their infants. The programs also generally emphasize
well-defined language-development procedures both in the
home and early childhood learning centers. Those programs
which are cognitively oriented, execute a structured format,
stress language enrichment, parental education, and
maintain very favorable caretaker-child ratios are more
successful in raising or "normalizing" the intelligence of
"disadvantaged" children and in sustaining these benefits
than are traditional preschool programs.

As we noted in our summary regarding infant education,
special consideration should be given to the developmental
psychology and culture of Afrikan American children when
preschool programs are being considered and implemented.
The accelerated psychophysical development of Black
children should be kept in mind including their special
nutritional needs. Children's needs for cultural identity and
consciousness are of first importance.

Afrikan-based content and materials should be utilized
whenever and wherever possible. An Afrocentric cultural
presence should be maintained in the learning center by
means of art, pictures, books, games, dances, music, oral
recitations, video shows, celebrations, rituals, dress, and

other activities. Caretakers and instructors should demonstrate a love and enthusiasm for things Afrikan and should model socially-appropriate Afrocentric interpersonal relations for their preschool population. The preschool center staff should be solidly educated in regards to Pan Afrikan/ Afrikan American history, culture, and psychohistory, and how the developmental educational-program is related to these factors and to the future goals of Afrikan peoples.

■

Notes

1. Mahler, M., Pine,. F., & Bergman, A. (1975). *The Psychology Birth of the Infant.* New York: Basic Books.
2. Clark, K., and Clark, M. (1958). Identification and References in Negro Children. In *Readings in Social Psychology,* E. Maccohy, et al., (eds.). New York: Holt.
3. Rice, P. (1987) *The Adolescent: Development, Relationships, and Culture.* 5th ed. Boston: Allyn and Bacon.
4. Harter, S., (1981) A New Self-report Scale of Intrinsic versus Extrinsic Orientation in the Classroom: Motivational and informational components. *Developmental Psychology,* 17, pp. 300-312.
5. *N.Y. Times,* January 9, 1991 from Suzanne Daley's article entitled "Little Girls Lose Their Self-Esteem on the Way to Adolescence, study finds."

Appendix A

General Stages of Infancy/Toddlerhood and Related Stimulative Learning Activities

Time Period	Effective Learning Activities
Birth to 6-8 weeks, (the imprint period); fundamental maternal-infant bonding.	With keen awareness of infant's limitations take special precautions not to overstimulate, prematurely "teach" or "rush" the infant. Letting infant set its own learning and interest paces — seek to promote quiet alertness by stimulating and being sensitive to his senses. Engage infant in contingency play, i.e., expose infant to situations where through their actions, they can cause specific changes in their environment in a consistent manner (e.g., twirling of mobile by kicking or waving arms); interactive play, e.g., peekaboo, making friendly faces, smiling, etc.; observation play — providing the infant with interesting sights and sounds. Play visual, touch, hearing, smell and movement games (*see suggested reading list in Appendix C,* e.g., Susan Ludington-Hoe); Express nurturing behavior, e.g., rocking and soothing behaviors which enhance the child's sense of trust, self-esteem and competence.
8-13 weeks Increased social behavior, "dialogue," visual and hand activities	The above-named stimulation games, bonding and body toning activities continue. The infant's attention is increasingly focused on hands and he responds readily to activities which stimulate his exer-

cising of his hands' functions. His hunger for dialogue can be stimulated and satisfied by vocal imitation, alternating or reciprocal vocal games, facial expressions, stimulative eye-contacts, gazing, intonational changes; maternal encouragement of attention to objects and events. Contingent games encourage baby's eye-hand coordination. Encourage baby's awareness of his body as a whole, of his body parts, and his body as a separate object in a world of objects.

4-7 months

Encourage infant's burgeoning interest in space, spatial relations, movement in space and desire to learn about people and things in his spatial environment. Continue enhancing infant's eye-hand coordination, visual ability by use of various toys, games and social interactions, stacking and nesting toys. Encourage infant's attention by presentation of patterned novelty. Engage in verbal patterning of imitative games. During this period the infant takes increasing pride in his own power, his direct power to influence and change his environment. His memory is growing by leaps and bounds. Opportunities for interaction, solitary, some structured and free play, opportunities for listening and vocalizing should be provided. A variety of "category games" (categorization by shape, size, etc.) games for building abstract thinking ability, naming activities, as well as age-appropriate visual, and sensory stimulation games will suffice to meet the demands of the infant's free-reigning curiosity around age 6 months. Toys and instruments which can be used as a means of manipulating other toys will help to enhance his budding need to utilize various mediums in order to indirectly influence or change his environment and to further exercise his expression of intentionality.

The infant has been interested in words from the beginning, but this period usually demonstrates a measurably enhanced interest in words and evidence of learning a lot about words. This tendency will accelerate during the following stages. If appropriately stimulated by linguistic interactions during the prior stages the infant may now be able to repeat two-syllable sounds, recognize the names of some objects, imitate some words or to say some real words. If not, don't fret. However, his budding interest in words should be satisfied by labeling and naming objects, talking about how they feel, their shapes, colors, sizes, etc. Talk about the things they are experiencing at the time. The reading of simple storybooks, well photographed and illustrated, the use of nursery rhymes as you engage in finger plays and clapping games with your infant may be quite linguistically enriching.

8-13 months

This is the period of noticeably accelerated motor skills development, hence activity and freewheeling exploration. Toys and social interactions which stimulate and satisfy these orientations should be generously provided. Interest in books, read-aloud stories, colorful periodicals, continue to whet the infant's linguistic appetite. Presenting, labeling and verbally elaborating on objects also help to build the infant's rapidly growing vocabulary and support his increasingly successful efforts to speak his first words (if this is not occurring at this time do not worry or push, some smart babies may not speak until around the age of two years). Imitating his early words can be helpful.

14 months - 2 years

The infant may begin to talk in earnest, that is, engage in two-way conversations. His acquisition of new words and phases is not only demonstrated by the expression and increasingly accurate and appropriate use of language, but by his increasing capacity to understand simple, direct instructions and ability to respond to a number of your questions. Read-aloud activities should continue apace.

The infant's imaginative abilities may begin to fully blossom occurring this period. Now he may begin to play make-believe or pretend games. His imagination, the source of creative and problem-solving activities, may be supported or boosted by toys, objects, social interactive relations, which allow him to actively express or act out imaginary scenarios. Concept words and concepts may be increasingly emphasized as the infant moves toward and into his second year (concept words may include such terms like, more - less, long - tall, up - down, cold - hot, etc.)

Second year

Imagination blossoms more vividly and linguistic growth is exceedingly rapid. Manipulative and coordinative activities receive increasing attention and exercise and attain new levels of complexity. These remarkably enhanced imaginative, linguistic and manipulative/coordinative capacities may be supported and accelerated by the provision of imaginative materials and activities (people and imaginative figures, toy vehicles, play kits, etc.) language development materials (storybooks, picture books nursery rhymes, alphabet books, paper and pencil, etc.), manipulative toys (sorting boxes, stacking toys, puzzles, etc.) science and mathematics aids(magnets, nature collections, magnifying glass, etc.), and construction materials (blocks, interlocking plastic or wood pieces etc.), support and accelerate a number of cognitive skills and abilities. Many toys and materials can be fashioned instead of purchased at great expense from stores. Many of the books in our suggested reading provide detailed instructions for the provision and construction of appropriate toys and materials.

Increased exposure to activities outside the home should be emphasized. So should exposure to written words, the concepts of color, size, shape, number, time and sequential relations.

Allow and encourage quiet concentration. Emphasize elaborative reading style. Make effective use of story time for language development, by asking "what" questions, providing informative feedback, incorporating expansions and providing corrective modeling of linguistic expression. "Word" and "sentence" play, the stressing of prepositions (e.g., "in," "behind" etc.), emphasizing and contrasting adjectives ("big" ball vs "small" etc.), using dramatic and manipulative play to engagingly demonstrate appropriate language usage and expand language comprehension are very much in order during this time and later.

Third year

This period continues "full speed ahead" the developmental trends of the prior period with increased power and added abilities and focuses of attention. The supportive activities of the prior period are continued with additional developmental-stage appropriateness and elaboration. "Interactive" (child, caretaker, and jointly initiated) multisensory learning and multi-skill mastery (e.g., spatial, perceptual, large and fine motor, expressive/artistic language mastery) will substantially help to maintain or enhance infant's all-round intellectual, personal, social and emotional development. These may include all types of reading and language arts activities (developmentally appropriate ones, e.g.,

scribbling, making circles, zigzag
lines, letters, etc); use of language,
toys and games (puzzles, card-
matching games, alphabet match-
ups, etc.): dramatic or make-believe
play (e.g., toy people, animals, puppets, doctor's and others, "professional" kits, play money, toy cards,
etc.), math activities (counting
games, number puzzles, recognizing
written numbers, measuring instruments e.g., measuring spoons, cups,
clocks, etc.); science (experiments
with water, seeds and plants, collections, etc.), art, musical and dramatic activities, travel and cultivated activities.

Note: Again we must caution the parent or caretakers
against "pushing" or overstimulating children. Attempting
"too much, too soon" will defeat your developmental
purposes. Encourage, support and reinforce ongoing and
developing positive interests, abilities and skills, gently
and non-threateningly evoke the child's interest in and
attention on new activities without prodding and going
against its "natural," developmental or "tolerative" grain.
Pushing the child to achieve without providing appropriate opportunities for academic, cultural, and social
emotional stimulation and support is not only not recommended, but if reckless will generally lead to non-produc-
tive and counterproductive results.

Appendix B

Selecting A Good Preschool

Because preschools differ along many important educational dimensions — such as facilities, school culture, pedagogical styles, quality of teaching staff and teaching styles, educational mission and ideology — choosing the right school for your child not only requires a thorough knowledge of the preschool you plan for him or her to attend, but that you are thoroughly familiar with his or her particular needs and whether the school can meet them.

Investigate the content and characteristics of the school program and find out through direct observation, conversation with administrators, teaching staff and other parents, if the program is actually and efficiently implemented in daily practice.

Good preschools share the following characteristics:

- provide a safe, clean, roomy environment; provide toys, recreational play and educational materials and equipment in appropriate numbers, varieties, age-levels and, in good repair.
- provide appropriate furnishings, an organized but not overly restrictive environment; a well-lit, temperature-regulated, active, but not overly-noisy, classroom environment.
- provide a rich and stimulating environment in which learning occurs through playful, social and instructional interaction; through structured interaction with the learning instruments, tools, toys and special activity areas.

- provide the children with opportunities to engage in productive group activities, to be a part of a group; to visit interesting places, to witness and participate in important entertainment, educational and cultural events/programs.
- provide a focus on the development of personal, social, attitudinal and attentional skills, "learning how to learn" skills, necessary for later academic success.
- provide firm, fair, consistent discipline according to clearly defined guidelines, rules and regulations, all clearly understood by parents, staff and the children. Discipline is not be physical or injurious to the child's positive self-esteem and self-concept. Staff is alert to children's activities so as to prevent or quickly curtail behavioral and conduct problems.
- provide smooth transitions from one classroom activity to another.
- provide a well-trained staff; a staff intimately knowledgeable of history, culture, and psychology of the children they teach and care for; a favorable student-to-teacher ratio; a staff which exhibits high expectations of its students and which consistently and accurately evaluates its educational outcomes and updates its methodology and knowledge through ongoing in-service training and/or conferences.
- permit, if not require, considerable parental involvement.

Appendix C

Recommended Reading List

Armstrong, T. 1987. *In Their Own Way: Discovering and Encouraging Your Child's Personal Learning Style.* Los Angeles: Jeremy Tarcher.

Armstrong, T., 1991. *Awakening Your Child's Natural Genius: Enhancing Your Child's Curiosity, Creativity and Learning Ability.* Los Angeles: Jeremy Tarcher.

Arnold, L. 1980. *Preparing Your Children for Science: A Book of Activities.* N.Y.: Schocken Books, Inc.

Benjamin, A., & Shermer, M. 1991. *Teach Your Child Math.* Los Angeles: Lowell House.

Bird, M. 1991. *Mathematics for Young Children: An Active Thinking Approach.* N.Y.: Rouledge, Chapman & Hall Inc.

Dargatz, J. 1991. *52 Simple Ways to Build Your Child's Self-Esteem and Confidence.* Nashville: Oliver Nelson.

Devine, M. 1991. *Baby Talk: The Art of Communicating With Infants and Toddlers.* N.Y.: Plenum Press.

Doman, G. 1990. *Teaching Your Baby to Read.* N.Y.: Evans & Co.

Doman, G. & Doman, I. 1991. *How To Teach Your Baby Math.* N.Y.: Evans & Co.

Einon, Dorothy. 1985. *Play With A Purpose: Learning games for children six weeks to ten years.* N.Y.: Pantheon Books.

Garber, S., Garber, M., and Spigman, R. 1990. *If Your Child Is Hyperactive, Inattentive, Impulsive, Distractible: Helping The ADD (Attention Deficit Disorder)/Hyperactive Child: A Practical Program for Changing Your Child's Behavior With and Without Medication.* N.Y.: Random House.

Hainstock, Elizabeth. 1971. *Teaching Montessori In The Home: The School Years.* New York: Penguin.

Hale-Benson, Janice. 1986. *The Black Child.* Baltimore, MD: Johns Hopkins University Press.

Howlett, Bud. 1991. *How To Choose The Best School For Your Child.* N.Y.: Self Publishing.

Jones, M. 1989. *Understanding Your Child Through Play.* N.Y.: Prentice Hall.

Kent, G., and Kalkstein, K. 1981. *Smart Toys: For Babies From Birth To Two.* N.Y.: Perennial Library.

Kimmel, Margaret, & Segel Elizabeth. 1983. *For Reading Out Aloud!: From Infancy To The Teens.* N.Y.: Dell.

Ledson, S. 1985. *Teach Your Child To Read In 60 Days.* N.Y.: Berkeley Books.

Lipson, Eden. *The New York Times Parents' Guide To The Best Books For Children.* N.Y.: Times Books.

Ludington-Hoe, Susan. 1987. *How To Have A Smarter Baby: The Infant Stimulation Program For Enhancing Your Baby's Natural Development.* N.Y.: Bantam Books.

Meisels, S., and Shonkoff, J. 1990. *Handbook of Early Childhood Intervention.* N.Y.: Free Press.

Oppenheim, Joanne; Brenner, Barbara, & Boegehold, Betty. 1986. *Choosing Books For Children: Choosing the right book for the right children at the right time.* N.Y.: Ballantine Books.

Radford, J. 1990. *Child Prodigies and Exceptional Early Achievers.* NY.: Free Press.

Savage, T. 1991. *The Ready-To-Read, Ready-To-Count Handbook: A School Readiness Guide For Parents and Preschoolers.* N.Y.: New Market Press.

Segal, M. 1985. *Your Child At Play: Birth to One Year.* N.Y.: New Market Press.

Shulman, M. 1991. *The Passionate Mind.* N.Y.: Free Press.

Simon, S., and House, L. 1989. *101 Amusing Ways To Develop Your Child's Thinking Skills and Creativity.* Los Angeles: Lowell House.

Stoppard, M. 1991. *Know Your Child: How To Discover and Enhance Your Child's Potential.* N.Y.: Ballantine Books.

Tettman, David. 1987. *Basic Montessori: Learning Activities For Under Fives.* N.Y.: St. Martins Press.

Tingey, C. 1989. *Implementing Early Intervention.* Baltimore: Paul Brookes Publishing, Co.

Trelease, J. 1989. *The New Read-Aloud Handbook.* N.Y.: Penguin.

Tuttle, C., and Paquette, P. 1991. *Thinking Games To Play With Your Children: Easy Ways To Develop Creative and Critical Thinking Skills.* Los Angeles: Lowell House.

Wilson, Amos. 1978. *The Developmental Psychology of the Black Child.* New York: Africana Research Publications.

Index